The Universe Within
Essence of Hinduism

Dr. Partha Rajagopal PhD

ISBN: 978-1492808282
ISBN-13: 1492808288

DEDICATION

To my mother, my sisters, my wife and my children

CONTENTS

ACKNOWLEDGMENTS

I would like to thank my life's experiences for being the inspiration behind realizing this book. I thank my motherland, India for giving me the needed insights into the spiritual realm during my younger days. I thank the land of the United States for teaching me a lot about rights, values and pursuing one's true potentials.

I thank my mother and sisters for being talented and being inspirational to me. This work is a reflection of their own inner visions that they never could share with the world.

Special thanks to my wife and children for encouraging me in my efforts.

I would like to specially thank Bruce Terrill, a renowned Karate expert, a man of many talents who has been a source of inspiration and encouragement in creating this work.

I want to thank everyone who owns this book and cherishes what it offers.

INTRODUCTION

Dear reader,

This book is a result of many layers of inner experience in my life. We live in a world of dualism. It is very clear to us. We know the opposites very well and they always seem far apart. We need extremes because we can only sense one because of the other. Light is in contrast to darkness. Hot is in contrast to cold. Everything is relative. In this relativistic referential framework, we are able to function and orient ourselves using a starting point, dimensions and scales to measure those dimensions. We use time to differentiate the past, present and the future. Everything appears along a linear scale. In this frame of view, we always seek a point of origin, a creator, a future course and an end, only because we are able to comprehend the Universe in a way that is comfortable to us.

Without references, we simply feel disoriented and confused. Yet we live in this world of references and relativistic contrast with abstract aspects. We still do not know what life really is. We cannot point exactly where our mind is or how big it is. We cannot tell for sure how consciousness appears. We know and feel gravity. Yet we cannot tell why it has to be there in the first place. We do not know where the feelings of happiness or sorrow or guilt arise from and why. Are they in the heart or in the brain? What are gut feelings then? In addition we also hear about God and the soul. If we have to know precisely what these are, we encounter a million definitions and a billion counter-questions. We live in the middle of several unknowns, which really belong to the realm where dimensions, points of origin and references do not have any meaning. We simply accept these aspects and continue to orient ourselves and walk along the hanging bridge of referential framework over the chasm of the unmanifest dimensions, whose depth we cannot fathom. We feel comfortable with things that are more concrete and leave the abstract to the philosophers and seers.

We categorize trees by how they look – their barks, trunks, shapes, branches, leaves, seeds and so on. There is little realization that the real core of the tree is subterranean, invisible, not following any orderly pattern, reaching in all directions and being the foundation on which the entire tree exists. We think trees are still and stationary. They grow wherever they sprout. Yet they have a moving part that is constantly seeking nutrients and water. Their roots move all the time, growing randomly and knowing where to find the resources to survive without any of the sense organs that we are so accustomed to. The root belongs to the world of the abstract where everything connects with the world imperceptibly. That is why it is able to break through the concrete, much to the annoyance of the homeowners.

I started my life in India and settled in the United States. I have spent approximately half my life on one side of the earth and the other half in a place that is on the opposite side of the planet. When it is day in one place, it is night in the other. In one, they drive on the left hand side of the road and in the other, on the right hand side. One is a land of history and ancient traditions that have managed to survive to the present age. The other one is a young nation, only about two centuries old and yet has leap-frogged over many others in terms of equality, right, freedom and technology. There is a lot of mutual interests in both cultures today, each one looking at the other for strengthening itself. In a way, both cultures are on the opposing extremes. My experience in both makes me see the contrast and the realization of being a bridge between both. I am comfortable in both systems, knowing enough about each one. I might be right handed. Yet I need both my right and left hands to function. I belong to both worlds now. I love my life's experience in the two contrasting environments and it has given me the opportunity to look at the world from a totally unique perspective.

I trained as an engineer and worked in the engineering industry for many years. The engineering field is built on the concrete and far removed from the abstract. Everything has to be measured, quantified and approximated. The word infinity does not belong to the world of engineering. It functions within the framework of dimensions, units, codes and specifications. Everything is documented, verified and repeated. The term, "for practical purposes" is well understood in the engineering world. A circle becomes a polygon with "almost" infinite number of sides. And one does not have to sweat about measuring the circumference of a circle using tedious means of dealing with infinite sides. All one needs is a way to locate the center and draw a diameter through it. The engineer will come up with the circumferential length using a formula. And engineering has helped the modern world reach frontiers unthinkable a couple of centuries ago. While we pride ourselves of being able to create mega-structures using the modern engineering tools and resources, we still do not know how the ancient Egyptians, Chinese, the Mayans and Indians created such grand monuments that have stood over centuries without any of the tools that we take for granted today. There was a different perspective and approach towards the world in their days that was more reliant on intuition rather than intellect. Intuition belongs to the inner dimensions of human consciousness. One has to close the eyes to reach into the power of intuition.

Even though I was trained and spoke the language of the engineers, the abstract always appealed to me. I am an artist and a writer. These two aspects arise from the depths of the abstract. Imagination is the wall on which they get painted. And the mind knows what imagination is and sometimes it does not know what reality is. It can switch from one state to the other imperceptibly.

In the process of seeing myself in between the concrete and the abstract, a new learning happened. It brought several realizations about everything I had come across in my life and had not really paid attention to. An understanding began to develop where I was able to sense and know the intent and meaning of many things that I had come across. This book is a result of such an understanding.

There are many books about Hinduism, Philosophy, Scriptures and practices. If I have to write something about this system, then it has to offer a unique perspective about it. It is like seeing thousands of beautiful pictures of a famous place. Every picture is unique in its own way. And yet, none of them can entirely convey everything about that place. Uniqueness arises out of inner experience. And I am able to offer that unique perspective that emerged entirely from my life experience and inner search. I have rendered them here in a sequence that appeared on its own. You are able to see the fundamental structure of Hinduism, through my eyes, as it appeared to me one layer at a time. You will understand what I mean here when you look at the titles of the chapters.

I did not have to think when I wrote this work. I just let it appear from within. I realized that thinking only delayed the process. Writing this book itself became a spiritual experience exposing me to the dimensions that are beyond what is visible and the realization that the Universe is much bigger than what we understand and that it is not separate from us, out there in what we call as "space". We exist in this Universe where we only refer to the matter that is visible. The infinity that contains all this is basically nothing. Every time when we look at the night sky, we can see that nothingness that is infinite and realize the first contrast of nothing and infinite right within each other. All the light and information that reaches our eyes is from the past, sometimes having happened billions of years ago, even before the solar system came into existence.

When contrasts merge, it is indeed a spiritual experience. The manifested being looks at the unmanifest and realizes the Universe within. This is the real essence of Hinduism that I am presenting through the pages of this book. One might see chaos and randomness everywhere. Yet everything tends to fall into order. And that order is based on fundamental structure that is not discernable easily. The Universe has both chaos and order side by side. Our spirit is like the seven notes of a musical instrument. Just those seven notes do not make a song. It is the random and yet orderly manipulation of those notes that creates wonderful music. Each one of us is a composition made up of these fundamental notes and each is unique. I welcome you to read through the pages and realize the essence of what I have presented.

The Universe has only answers. Drop the questions and simply seek the answers and they will emerge from within.

Dr. Partha Rajagopal

2 THE MOUNTAIN

Imagine a snowcapped mountain or mountain range in a tropical or sub-tropical place. When we think of the tropics, we immediately associate it with a hot climate, lush vegetation, animals and abundance. One does not associate snow with a tropical place. Yet there are mountains that have their bases in the tropical climate and their summit is covered with glaciers. India's climate ranges from the tropical to sub-tropical. Its entire northern edge is bordered by the snow capped Himalayas. The presence of this mountain range has allowed for India to develop its own unique religious and cultural system remaining uninterrupted for most of its history. All invasions into India have happened through the narrow passages along its Northwestern edge. Whatever groups came into India simply became assimilated and absorbed by the existing system. The geography has shaped the land's history into its own uniqueness.

The Himalayas are made up of sedimentary rocks that were at the bottom of an ancient ocean. One cannot imagine a deep ocean bottom emerging into the tallest mountain ranges in the world. Though it happened over millions of years, it happened. Even the bottom of the ocean one day can become the top of the world. Contrast is difficult to imagine. It sounds like someone's fantasy. The Himalayas defines the very basis of Hinduism – one end of the extreme becoming the other end. The Himalayas are the classic example of the extremes coming together – the ocean bottom turning into a mountaintop. One of the ancient fossils (ammonite) and whalebones began to confirm the theory that the Himalayas were once the bottom of an ocean. The ammonite fossil is considered a Divine element in some Hindu cults (Saligram). It is placed at the altar and prayed to in some places.

The mountain is a universe unto itself. Its base is wide. Along its slopes lies dense vegetation. All kinds of creatures live amongst the vegetation. Farm lands stretch from the base all the way across to the horizon. At the base, many trails and pathways can be found. Some are rough and steep. Some are well paved. If one were to climb the mountain without anything on his hands and has to rely on what the mountain offers to survive, it can be quite challenging. If he does not have any weapon to protect him or has no tools on his hands, it makes his task even more daunting. But that is how the ancient people lived. Many became familiar with their paths and ventured only along those paths. They knew every twist and turn on those paths, the best time to use them and knew about the potential dangers. If several people decide to climb a mountain whose pathways are uncharted and if none of them carried anything with them, they are first going to choose the path based on their own physical condition.

A heavy person might choose a path that is sloping gently with many spots to rest along the way, having access to water. An older person might seek a similar pathway as well that is wide and safe, knowing well that his journey would take a very long time. A young and energetic individual might like to reach the top quickly and be the first one to get there. He might like challenges on the way. Someone may not even want to take the effort to go up at all. Everyone is different. Everyone might find that path that is suitable for his or her journey to the top. And there is no obligation to go up. One can choose to stay down below and be content. No one knows why some people are curious to experience being at the summit.

The base of the mountain is so wide that there are plenty of paths available. One has the chance to choose a path to start with. As one ascends upwards, he finds that he needs to make more efforts. The pull of gravity can be tiring. It becomes easier to fall and roll down and more difficult to climb. Every step during a climb needs effort while falling does not. He sees everything naturally tending to go downwards. The rocks on the slopes have rolled down. The rivers and streams always flow down. Rain falls down. But the clouds inspire him. They seem to reach the summit effortlessly by becoming lighter. They seem to defy gravity somehow. The birds are able to swing their wings and fly high in every direction. The trees are comfortable along the slopes by firmly rooting themselves. Inspired by those aspects that tend to go against the pull of gravity, the climbers go further.

Beyond a certain point, it is very discouraging. Finding food and water becomes harder. This is the point many give up. Many tell themselves they have had enough and it is not worth going up any further. The legs are begging. The body cannot take it. Every step seems to take a monumental effort. The mind begins to act in a very strange way. Beyond this point, only those who are mentally tough can proceed. The mountain is not to be underestimated. Arrogance and immaturity can lead to a steep fall. The climate on a mountain at higher altitudes can be unpredictable. More people can fall from a higher elevation. Only those who want to risk it all and persevere can go further. At the base many thousands started out. As the elevation became higher and higher, the different paths starting at the base begin to merge. There are only fewer paths available and only fewer people are able to go further.

Once the timberline is crossed, it becomes like a desert. Food is scarce. Climate is harsh. Weather is unpredictable. Endurance becomes questionable. Now is the time guides can be of great help. Guides are those who have been to the summit many times and have understood the mountain well. They know how to get there and what not to do. Without the guide, climbing can be quite challenging, especially if one started out with nothing as precondition at the beginning. The guide first trains the climbers in every way possible. One has to trust the guide. It is not that everyone uses the guides. Some do manage to reach the summit on their own efforts. But once they have achieved that, they want to return there more often. Something inside them wants them to approach the summit. And as one nears the summit, he realizes that the thousands of paths that started out around the base of the mountain have all merged into one. There is only one summit and there is only one path left at the very end.

The view from the summit is very different from that of the base. From the summit, one sees in all directions, as far as the horizon can allow. The mountain is rooted on the ground. Yet its summit is in the heavens. One who can traverse from the base to the summit can relate to this uniqueness. A mountain links the two extremes of the sky and the earth. It becomes the gap between the two. By entering the gap, a climber is able to reach the summit and realize the whole earth around.

A mountain appears stable and unmoving. Relative to the human dimensions, the mountain is gigantic. It outlasts the human life span. It can take on the thunder and stop the clouds. It can take on the storm and drain it down along its slopes. It sustains all kinds of life forms. It can be inanimate, but a mountain is a world unto itself. When a mountain shakes, the human knows what it is like. Standing at the base of a mountain and experiencing the vision of it filling the view from one end to the other and the top hidden in the clouds can be a humbling and ego crushing experience. A mountain in its full majesty overwhelms the human. It kindles a spiritual feeling deep inside. One respects a mountain for what it is. Humans have defined the Divine in its own dimensions. Many see it as ever lasting, powerful, benevolent, unmoving, unchanging, and free of limited emotions. A mountain seems to meet most of these characteristics when compared to the humans in all these aspects. Based on our own definition, the mountain does become Divine.

Mountains are considered auspicious in Hindu religious systems. The Himalaya (means "The abode of snow") is revered. It is from where the holiest of holy rivers in Hinduism, The Ganga (Ganges in English) emerges. It is home to many holy places and shrines. It is home to many yogis and Siddhas. It is considered mystical and magical. Himalaya is considered as the head of the Indian sub-continent. It is the abode of Shiva who meditates in silence.

All across the Indian sub-continent, mountains and hills are revered. One always finds a temple at the top of each mountain or hill. Mountains and caves are the refuge sought by yogis to practice deep meditation. The whole structure of Hindu religions resembles that of a mountain. As one reads on, this structure will become more evident.

2 THE LION

There was once a sincere spiritual seeker. He meditated for many years and observed the hardest penance. His desire was to get the vision of Lord Vishnu, the protector of the Universe and get His blessings and a boon. He did not lose heart. He had unshakeable faith. He spent many years in hard penance and pushed himself to the edge of his very existence. And one day it happened. He could not believe his eyes! His eyes could not even look at the dazzling brilliance that appeared in front of him. He could see no end to it. He could not define it. But he realized that the One he prayed to, stood in front of him.

"Speak to me my beloved son, I am here for you," said a gentle voice.

The pious man could not speak. He sobbed profusely. He was overwhelmed by the joy of what he was going through. He wanted this Divine moment to stay on forever. Somehow he gathered his strength. He wanted to be an immortal so. that he could be in the body and be in the blissful experience forever. That is the only thing he had known. He could not utter it immediately.

"Immortality does not mean existing forever in a mortal body my son," said the voice. "You need to transcend the limitation of the body."

It did not need the verbal utterance of his wish. He began to shake. This Divine being knows everything. He did not know any other way of remaining in bliss. He had been born in a body. He could not think of existing without a body and be blissful at the same time. He pondered how he could make his wish heard by changing the request. He realized he could do that. The Divine never denies a wish. It waits until the wish is granted. With humbleness he began to speak.

"Oh my Lord! Oh my life! Oh the ever lasting and ever present one! This mortal body will perish one day. But let it not perish under the following circumstances. It will not be killed by a human or a non-human, ever. It will neither die during the day nor during the night. It will not die inside my mansion or outside of it." How clever? How can these conditions ever become true? Even the Divine could not refuse this wish. It has no choice but to grant it.

"So be it," said the voice and suddenly everything disappeared. The man sobbed and sobbed for having that incredible experience. He realized that the Divine did not object to his clever wish. It worked. There was no way the conditions he had laid could be met. He was, for all practical purposes, an immortal. Nothing could kill him. This meant he could meditate and be in that blissful state for as long as he wanted. Or, he could be the Lord of the world for sometime. Why not? His spiritual humbleness suddenly was replaced by ego at an instant. Even after crossing the barrier of ego, it does not die. It can resurface with a vengeance. It became so strong that the man laughed uncontrollably. Bliss or being the most powerful? Everything was to be his. Why not? He could always return to penance and bliss whenever he wanted. He was going to live forever. Why not just enjoy being powerful for sometime? His ego made the choice.

Many years went and the man became all-powerful. He made his subjects submit to his whims. Nothing could defeat him. His surging ego silenced the sense of guilt that kept reminding him about abusing his power slowly. It took him to a level where he began to believe that being all mighty and powerful was what his destiny was. He felt at some point that he had become Divine himself. That is what

Divine is – all-powerful and immortal. He was one among the Gods. There was no more need to worship any God when he became one himself. He was God and every one of his subjects had to know this truth. Nothing could stop him - not even the Being that granted him his wish.

Destiny always finds a way out of everything. Cleverness is human. It works well up to some extent. Beyond that, the most impossible probability can happen. He had a beloved son. He could make all his subjects submit to his will, except for his son who had an unshakeable faith in the real divine who had granted his father the boon itself. He prayed for his father and pleaded for mercy and forgiveness for his deeds. He knew that his poor father had been blinded by his ego. The mighty king could not stomach this rebellious faith in his own son. The world would laugh at him. The only thing that was preventing him from crushing this young boy was his overwhelming affection for him. He was still a mortal and was not beyond emotions. He did everything he could to convince his son that he had become God himself and the God that could be tricked was inferior in every way. His son could not be convinced.

One evening he sent away everyone from his palace and then he confronted his son.

"Son, ask your God to appear in front of me now. I want to ask Him why He is afraid of me,"

"Father, the One that created everything, does not fear anything. He has only eternal love for you because you are His child too"

"If I can trick Him and become immortal as a result, then this Being is not all that powerful as we all think. Human intelligence wins over everything. That is why all these years It has gone into hiding. He will not face me again because even He cannot destroy me. You will have to accept this reality"

"Father, Please do not challenge the all pervading Divinity. You are its reflection too. For my sake, please do not try to supersede its power"

"Power?" he laughed loud. "Do you realize my power? I just want to test the power of this All Mighty. I know I became immortal through the boon it granted. But I fooled It. I can fool It again. So bring Him here. Where is He?"

"Father, He is everywhere"

"Really? Everywhere? But hiding from me! Because He made a mistake of being tricked by me. He is embarrassed, isn't He? Let me see. May be He is hiding inside this pillar. Let me break that down and see if He is inside of it"

His son fell at his feet pleading him not to challenge the Divine. But the mighty king was not afraid. What could kill him? A human? A non-human? Inside the palace? Or outside? During the day? Or during the night? Which condition will make him a mortal again?

He began to smash the pillar. The pillar could not withstand his power. It began to crumble and fall apart. Dust filled the air as the pillar crumbled and fell to pieces. When the dust cleared, a strange creature stood where the pillar was. It had a human body with the head of a male lion. It looked ferocious and angry. As it stepped out, he was suddenly worried about his son. He knew he was immortal. But his son could not see a scary being of this kind. He ran and hid his son behind his back.

He took his weapon and hurled it at the creature. The weapon hit the creature and fell to the side without causing a scratch on it. It began to advance towards him. Every weapon thrown at the creature made no impact on it. It kept advancing towards him, roaring with rage. Its eyes were glowing red. He picked up his son and ran to the entrance of his palace. He left him outside and told him to stay there until he was done dealing with this creature.

The creature caught hold of him at the entrance of the palace as he tried to enter it. The man realized how mightily powerful this creature was. Its roar was deafening. He found it hard to wrestle. He began to feel excruciating pain as the creature began to tear his skin.

Its jaws gripped his neck and bite it down. He realized he could not breathe. He sensed that he was dying. He could not believe what was happening to him. How was this possible? The creature lifted him and put him on its lap. It sat at the entrance of the palace – neither inside, nor outside. He found himself too weak to fight it anymore. When the day ended and night began, the creature took his life. It was twilight time, neither day nor night.

Finally the mortal met his end at the hands of this creature, which was neither human nor a non-human. All his cleverly created conditions had been met. The ferocious creature tore up his belly, pulled out his guts and wore it as a garland around its neck. Blood spilled everywhere. His son, seeing all this went motionless in shock. All he could do was pray for peace and pray for calmness. He prayed for forgiveness. He closed his eyes and prayed.

When he opened his eyes, he saw this blissful Being standing in front of him. The half human – half lion creature had disappeared. The Being was full of unconditional love. He could see his father fully merged into It. He realized that the Being was Lord Vishnu Himself who had come to save his father from being destroyed by his own ego. By merging with the Divine, his father had indeed become one with It and immortal. All he could do was to merge with that bliss and be in that state of joy.

Thus ends the story of the man, who met the Divine when the extremes came together – inside and outside, day and night, human and non-human. Though his mortal end was violent, he could transcend the mortal state and merge with the immortal presence.

Immortality does not mean existing in a body forever. It is experiencing life eternally without having to be born in a body again.

3 THE ELEPHANT

There are many ways of observing an elephant, especially when everyone around is visually impaired. We have to rely on kinesthetic and auditory senses to construct an understanding of what it is. If we are lacking visual capability, we won't even know what an image means. The same goes for anything that we observe. All our observations are based on what we have come across so far in our lives.

A world that was used to seeing organized religions, one day suddenly encountered the Indian sub-continent. A religion, according to their perception, had a founder, at least a God or two, a scripture or holy book of edicts and codes of conduct, a system of religious officials and institutions that maintained the integrity and continuity of the religion. Everything else was primitive and did not belong to the civilized world. In India, they encountered many Gods, many scriptures, many religious leaders, and countless number of temples, belief systems that ranged from primitive to incomprehensible pagan practices, naked fakirs and complete lack of any structure. They simply could not comprehend something that they saw the way it was. If they had the monumental task of having to teach the barbarians what religion is, they did not know where to start.

As a result, the system survived over the centuries by simply being complex and incomprehensible to everyone, sometimes even including those who were its followers. In order to characterize it for an easier approach towards understanding, the whole thing was put hurriedly into something that resembled their own religious systems. Modern Hinduism was born. Every small religious group in India sees Hindus as people who are not Christians or Muslims or Jains or Sikhs or Buddhists. That makes it a simpler definition. Everything that is not a recognizable religion in the Indian subcontinent can be viewed as a belonging to a miscellany called Hinduism, a religion now defined by that which is "Not" rather than that which "is".

There are more than a 1.2 billion citizens in India today. Out of that, at least about 1 billion citizens call themselves Hindus. If one were to ask each one what Hinduism is, and compiled it all, he would find a billion descriptions of it, with overlaps of their perception everywhere. If one were to ask me what Hinduism is, my humble answer is this – There is no such thing as Hinduism. We all know Islam, Christianity, Judaism, and Buddhism as world's great religions today. Then there are many religions with smaller number of followers across the globe. They all have a structure that I have mentioned above and are relatively recent religions. Where does Hinduism fit? It has close to a billion followers or at least those who claim to belong to that system.

Hinduism is like a cloud. Seen from a vast distance, it has a shape and color to it. As one approaches it, it becomes harder and harder to feel or touch anything. One gets lost in it. What we call as Hinduism today has undergone several cycles of morphing over the eons.

The term "Hindu" is not a religious one. In reality, it is a geographical term denoting the denizens of the Indian sub-continent. The Arabs called it "Al Hind", the land that lay to the East of the river Sindh, which now runs through the nation of Pakistan that derives its identity from two bases – Islam and not being a Hindu. The Greeks called the river as Indus when they ventured that far from their homeland in the past. The name India is derived from the Greek name Indus for the river Sindh. Similarly the name Hindu is derived from the Arabic name Al Hind. Thus the term "Hindu" is as geographical as the word European or American or Chinese. India is the only place on earth where geography and religion are denoted by the same name. While the geographical name is real, the religious name is only mythical.

When I am about to describe the essence of Hinduism, I need to make it very clear what I am going to address. I am not going to address anything that deals with a religion that really does not exist. I am going to look at the fundamental aspects of the various religious systems that coexist in India that share a common ground. This commonality is not apparent, just like the essence of anything needs to be extracted through some effort. I am going to pick bits and pieces from the different religious systems to construct my narration in this book.

Here is the one-billionth definition of "Hinduism" – mine. I find it a lot easier to deal with it by changing the name to "Hindu religions" (religions belonging to the land of Al Hind). Thus I can keep the geographical and religious entities apart and the meaning of the terms would make sense. This is like clubbing the three modern religions – Judaism, Christianity and Islam into a group called "Semitic religions." They share a lot of things – geographical, prophets, stories, their scriptures, holy places etc. and yet differ from each other. Similarly, Hindu religions are those, which originated in the land of Indians, who live to the East of the river Sindh. There are many religions and sects that exist in modern India. They are religions on their own merit. In my view, they all are Hindu religions (religions born in Al Hind). There is Jainism, Buddhism, Sikhism, Vaishnavism, Shaivism, and many other religions, along with cults based on mother Goddess (Shakti, Kali), animistic systems and many others that do not fit into any of the above categories.

India also is home to at least seven systems of philosophy that range from atheism to abstract views of the world. There are scriptures that justify discrimination based on one's birth to a very profound contemplation of God and the Universe. India is home to every extreme one can perceive. Extremes coexist. Where extremes come together, it helps transcend into the realm of the Divinity. In the book, "Freedom at Midnight" written by Dominic Lapierre and Larry Collins[1], they look at this nation as it gained its independence from the British in 1947. They wonder how a nation where one set of people writes from left to right and another group that writes from right to left can coexist and survive as a nation. Interestingly they have done that very thing over many decades, albeit occasional friction and readjustments. India is a land of extreme contrasts and this contrast defines the essence of the Hindu system.

What I am presenting through the following pages is going to be somewhat different from what everyone else has been doing. I do not see the need to define everything and provide a clear view of the Hindu religious system. If I start doing that, I am afraid there will be a billion more books written for the same purpose by everyone who thinks he or she knows better. There are detailed books that deal with different religious and philosophical texts from India. I will confine my presentation to the way I have perceived this great elephant, however impaired I might be, using my experience and observations. I have tried hard to avoid turning this work into a tourist guide for the unwary travelers who step into India.

Talking about the elephant, it is always a custom and tradition in Southern India to start with a prayer to Lord Ganesh. Ganesh goes by many names – Ganesha, Ganapathy, Vignesh, Vinayak and so on. Most Hindu temples in Southern India have altars for Lord Ganesh. He has the head of an elephant and an obese human body.

A mouse is always associated with Ganesh. The mouse stands nearby. People would break coconuts in front of the altar, praying for His blessings to get through exams, get marriage alliances to succeed, land a job and so on. If it happens, some devotes would return and break coconuts as promised.

During my childhood years, I would always keep an eye on the Ganesh temples around. There were some at the street corners as well. When coconuts were shattered, I would jump in with many others to grab a piece for myself. That was an age when I did not worry much about the meaning behind everything. For a child, everything is a fun play. The blessing was in the coconut piece as far as I was concerned. I would sometimes go around the Ganesh temple 108 times in the evenings with some childish wish.

I seldom thought about what Ganesh meant or what the significance of the number 108 was. I never pondered about the breaking of the coconut or the little mouse that was always there in every Ganesh temple. We know that children feel the same about Santa Claus for a few years, until it dawns on them that mommy and daddy were clandestinely packing gifts and leaving them next to the Christmas tree every year. Once they become aware that Santa Claus actually originates from a departmental store, their childhood innocence is lost. But they still like the gifts near the Christmas tree, even after they grow up. I began to think about why these traditions and beliefs came into being and what they were achieving. This book is a culmination of such realizations that began to unravel on their own. Let me start with a prayer to Ganesh, for me and you the reader that this book be an enjoyable one that enlightens both myself and you into knowing more about not only the Hindu system, but also about the similarity between it and whichever system you believe in.

The elephant was an important aspect of ancient India. Every temple had elephants. Some still do. Elephants were used during wars to knock down barricades and giant entrances, wreak havoc amongst enemy lines and carry the kings and generals. Elephants were also used as vehicles for hunting. They were used for moving heavy loads, and in the construction of massive granite temples that adorn Southern India. The elephant formed an important part of temples.

Today it has become quite expensive to sustain elephants and as a result, they have disappeared from most temples.

4 THE COW

Everything starts from the street. The rich might live in the mansions and the poor in their ghettos. But both rich and poor have to come through the streets to go wherever they are going.

The view from the street looks very different to that from inside every home. In the street, everyone follows the unwritten codes of conduct. Inside their homes, they are free to do what they like. It is their kingdom. On the street rules come into picture.

Every home is located and identified by the street it is in. Without the street, your home has no identity and the mail does not arrive. The street defines the map and the map defines the world. A Street is the only way to find a home.

And there is a street view of everything. People have opinions and beliefs that they share at the street level. What most people have known or heard about Hinduism is at the street level. This is almost true for every system. There are a handful of real experts who really know and the rest think they are experts without really knowing anything. At the street level, a person who has evolved in this system is familiar with the trinity of supreme Gods – Brahma, Vishnu and Shiva. One is associated with generation, one with operation and the last one with dissolution. Everything appears, exists and disappears. Day appears, prevails and disappears into the night, only to reappear again. This cyclical nature is well recognized in every Hindu system and is known at the street level itself. The three Lords are associated with their consorts, Saraswati, Lakshmi and Parvati. Saraswati carries wisdom, Lakshmi is all wealth and Parvati is valor. The Gods have their own families and children.

Ganesh is the son of Shiva and Parvati. According to mythology, Ganesh had the normal human head. One day, Parvati asked her son to stand guard outside so that she could bathe. Shiva came to see her and Ganesh would not let Him in. In anger, Shiva severed his son's head off. When Parvati came out, she saw her son lying headless. Shiva realized what he had done and in order to keep the domestic peace alive, found an elephant, cut its head and installed it in his son's neck. Ganesh recovered. However he had to exist with the head of an elephant. Thus goes the story of Ganesh on the street. It is very entertaining to hear it as a kid. Most of us heard many such mythical stories told by people on the street. Sometimes they would be our bedtime stories narrated by grandmothers and aunts. Much like Disney stories where animals take human characteristics, mythological stories fulfilled the same needs for us. If one left the story at the street level, it stays there. But if one entered the temple of wisdom from the street, the story takes a different dimension. I will come to that later in this book.

India's mythology inter-connects all the Gods, the Demigods, Goddesses, sages, saints, and kings in their never ending quest against the evil. When a spiritual seeker begins to gain ascendancy, the Demigods begin to test them. Many a times, such seekers fail the test and fall. The evil does not appear out of nowhere. Some turn evil and cannot be contained by mere mortals. It needs Divine intervention. We saw this in the story of Nara-Simha, the lion headed God earlier. Animals play an important part in many mythical stories. The most revered animal that is mentioned even in the sacred texts of the Hindu system, the Vedas, is the cow.

The Sanskrit word for the cow is "Go" or "Gow". For thousands of years, the cow has been revered as the real wealth in India. Every cow gives the essential materials for survival – milk, butter, melted butter, butter milk, meat, leather, plowing the field, tilling the land, drawing carts, and its dung became the fuel for cooking food. No other animal gave that much sustenance to the people who relied on farming and agriculture. India's largest industry is agriculture even to this day. Cow is associated with wealth. In the past, one's status depended on the number of cows he owned. Temples were granted with cows by kings and chieftains.

The street is also where one finds cows in India. While buses, trucks, cars, bicycles, rickshaws, carts, people and everything else move through the streets of India, the one that generally finds rest on the busy streets is the cow. The hurry and speed on the roads do not bother them. The barrage of honks does not perturb them. Cows amble through busy roads unaffected by all the mayhem around them.

The cow symbolizes peaceful existence. Cows are quite docile in nature. They mind their own business and do not show aggression in general. If one looks at a cow sitting quietly in a street full of chaotic noise and traffic, it can bring the feeling of calmness in adversity. Anyone who is calm amidst chaos and turbulence is unaffected by it and can act with clarity. The cow symbolizes that inner calmness that everyone is seeking. Cows also symbolize tolerance. They undergo considerable abuse and yet keep giving. Cows give everything for our sustenance. Anything that gives is regarded as Divine. Being calm, tolerant and giving, the cow symbolizes Mother Earth who takes all our abuse and yet only gives. The cow thus forms a very important element in the Hindu belief system. Eating beef is a taboo in today's Hindu tradition.

Krishna, the Divine incarnation of Lord Vishnu, is known as Gopal. "Go" refers to the cow and "Pal" refers to the one who maintains them. He is also called as Govardhana or Govinda. Just like Jesus, who was addressed as the shepherd, Krishna is addressed as the keeper of the cows. When emperors built massive temples in the past, they were provided with elephants, cows, priests and land. The system was self-sustaining while ardent devotees provided monetary help through alms and donations. The cow becomes an integral part of worship in most Hindu temples.

Both the cow and the elephant symbolize the Earth. Cow represents the tolerant, ever giving nature of the earth, while the Elephant represents the heaviness of the state of being grounded. We exist on the ground, the surface of the earth. The elements of the earth, which give us stability and sustenance, are in the elephant and the cow, which form an integral part of Hindu temples. Ground is where one starts. Ground also represents the street. To enter a temple or a church or any place of worship, one enters from the street. If one is aware of the starting point while entering a place of worship, it sets up the necessary vibes needed to immerse oneself in devotion.

The Hindu system insists on one being grounded at all times, especially in places of worship. The feet have to be bare and feel the ground as one walks into a temple. People are discouraged from foot ware inside homes as well. Though at the street level it is known as being respectful, the inner meaning of it is to feel the ground we stand on. Any spiritual quest starts at the ground level where we all exist as human beings. We cannot remain detached from it for too long. In the past, the denizens of India seldom wore slippers or shoes. It will become clear when we approach the topic of Chakras and how they are kept active by following religious and social codes of conduct. Walking barefoot inside a Hindu temple is one of those codes. Offering respect to the cow and the elephant also enhance the cleansing of the Chakra that is related to the ground. The significance of walking barefoot, the cow and the elephant can be discerned from the system of Chakras. The only people who wear slippers in such an environment are the yogis who have a specific reason not to be grounded. They wear wooden slippers.

Everything in the Hindu religious systems is related to the Chakras and ethereal meridians in the human body known as the "Nadi". Every ritual, every symbol, every myth, every name of the God or Goddess are all related to the Chakras and Nadis. The essence here is that we are starting at the ground level or from the street where ignorance prevails. Ignorance is bliss according to the sages. Humans at this level tend to follow stories and myths with full faith in an almost childlike manner. It is a good starting point. The street is where the home is. And one can only enter the home from the street.

Spiritual accomplishment happens when one realizes his inner home. And it always starts at the street level. Everything at the street level is conveyed indirectly and metaphorically so that one does not have to think or analyze much at the start. One does not have to be an expert in the first grade. So if people worship the cow, pay respect to the elephant by breaking coconuts and remove their slippers out of respect, it is meant for a purpose that is not known to them directly. The important thing is to try to enter one's home and not preferring to stay on the street. Everyone has that inner desire to find his or her own home.

5 THE SERPENT

Almost every deity in the Hindu religious system is associated with a snake. Shiva wears a necklace made up of snake.

Shiva depicted with a serpent around His neck

Lord Vishnu is depicted as lying on a bed made up of a curled, multi-headed snake. The snake, especially the cobra has been revered across various cults and groups since ancient times in India. Snake represents manifestation in the form of energy. That which moves on its own, is alive. Snake symbolizes the state of aliveness. In the Hindu belief system, energy is depicted in a female form – Shakti. We know today that energy moves in the form of waves. We can only see energy moving when matter moves as energy sweeps through it. Life energy sweeps through us, who are made up of matter. The snake depicts the wavy movement of energy. That which is alive is conscious. Even the Gods Shiva, Vishnu and Brahma become mere states unless Shakti vibrates through them. Snake worship symbolizes worshipping life itself. In the humans, life current runs so long as Shakti resides at their root Chakra. She goes by the name "Kundalini" and is depicted as a coiled serpent. We are still on the street level. We will get to know more as we begin to enter the place of worship we call the home.

The snake, which undergoes the molting of its skin, represents the cycle of death and rebirth. Old skin is cast off and new one is taken. The snake hunts for the rodents that hide underground. The mouse is always shown next to Lord Ganesh, where it symbolizes the conscious mind that keeps wandering in all directions. By consuming the mind, Kundalini, symbolized by the snake, emerges out of her dormant realm. The elephant, the snake and the rodent belong to the ground state of existence. So long as the elephant's foot stands between the snake and the rodent - the mind, and the Kundalini, ordinary existence prevails where we live relying on our five senses and do not see anything beyond. Prayer to the elephant headed Lord Ganesha, can allow that elephant foot to lift and let the snake, Kundalini, to consume the rodent, the mind. Much effort is needed to make this elephant lift its foot.

In essence, the cow represents the all giving and nurturing mother Earth; the snake represents the life that has emerged out of mother earth; the rodent represents the wandering mind, that lives in fear and is consumed by life; the elephant represents the grounding of living beings on earth. All are interconnected and interdependent. God is simply the state of this consciousness and existence.

6 THE EAGLE

We are simply observing everything mostly at the street level. A lot of groundwork is needed before we can enter the abode. The worldview of Hindu religions is based on what has been observed on the streets and from above. To see the inside of the homes, one has to enter them. And we will do so as soon as we become ready for it. A map view gives a very quick and generic idea about something from a distance. The world has no time to spot each and every detail, much like an eagle, which soars above and looks at everything from a height. But the eagle only looks for its prey from above. It has sharp vision and can spot its prey from a high elevation. The bird sees the streets and knows the map and orientation from the height.

That which can see from above and get an overall picture of everything is the intellect. The eagle represents the intellect. It hunts the snake, which represents the instinct based existence. Intellect dominates the instinct in humans to a large extent. Lord Vishnu, who represents the state of human consciousness, rides the eagle and sleeps on the serpent. This is symbolic of the human consciousness relying on the intellect while the instinct runs in the background. Vishnu is depicted as lying on a serpent, which describes the inner mind, and the reliance on the senses for basic survival. Intellect goes beyond the senses, soaring upward in analytical ability and contemplation. The human state of consciousness (Vishnu) functions with the two extremes – intellect and instinct (the eagle and the serpent).

The eagle and the snake are adversaries. A snake can bite an eagle and kill it. An eagle can pounce on a snake and take it away. Under Lord Vishnu they are depicted together. Divine experience can bring the extremes together. When extremes merge or become balanced, duality disappears.

The eagle attacks both the snake and the rodent. Intellect always tries to break free of animal instinct. The eagle does not belong to the ground. Intellect is something the humans are gifted with. And it always triggers this passion of venturing into the unknown. There is a story of Gajendra, the elephant getting its foot trapped by a crocodile. When Gajendra screams, Lord Vishnu hurries to save him from the crocodile. He rides on his Eagle, which is holding the snake in its claws. This was a standard bedtime story told by grandmothers to children during the good old days. Vishnu unleashes his weapon, the spinning blade that kills the crocodile and releases the foot of the elephant. This simply depicts the removal of bondage to desires. When the extremes are together (the eagle and the snake or the intellect and the instinct), the Divinity within arises and helps cut off all the bondage from earthly desires (the elephant representing the earthly state and the crocodile the desires), thereby liberating an aspiring spiritual seeker from bondage.

In essence, the eagle represents the free willing intellect that wants to explore and know that truth that is behind everything; as it does, it has to liberate itself from the state of being grounded, which is represented by the elephant. When it does, fear disappears as life and awareness expand, represented by the snake held by the eagle's claws; In that state, bonds and earthly ties, represented by the crocodile that pulls even an elephant down, are broken by the Divine experience.

7 THE SWAN, THE BULL AND THE MONKEY

God is depicted as three separate entities in the Hindu system – Brahma being associated with creation or generation, Vishnu with operation and sustenance and Shiva with dissolution. The three are states of consciousness through which we travel across in our lifetime. We arise from a creative stage and live a full life and then we depart. At the street level there is no realization that if we utilize the living stage into transcending the departing stage, we can connect with the source of creation, which is full of awareness and wisdom.

The sleeping Vishnu depicts our autonomous system that is running our entire body in the background whether we are awake or asleep or unconscious. The heart is pumping blood, the various systems in the body – the digestive, the elimination, the respiratory, the immune system and so on are functioning continuously whether we are aware or not. This is symbolized by a sleeping Vishnu on a bed of life depicted by the snake. The snake floats in a cosmic ocean, indicating the connectivity between the individual and the universe at the fundamental level.

Words, by themselves cannot express an experience fully. But stories can metaphorically allude to the underlying experience. And in a story, animals play an important part in depicting the various aspects in our lives. One would find different animal statues accompanying the deities in every temple. Every deity is associated with specific set of animals. Vishnu has the eagle and the serpent.

Shiva has the bull as his vehicle. Brahma is associated with the white swan.

The Swan is denoted by the words "Hamsa" in Sanskrit. "Ham" is a base sound attached to a Chakra. We will go over the Chakras in detail at a latter chapter. In the yogic tradition in India, the title "Hamsa" is always given to someone who has become self-realized. One who has gone past even this stage and is always in Divine consciousness is known as "Parama Hamsa". Swan represents wisdom. One who reaches this stage is full of awareness and is directly linked to the fundamental aspect of the Universe. He or she has realized the Brahma within. Such a person is called Brahman. A Brahman is said to have been born twice – once in the physical body at the human consciousness level and once more after attaining the Divine Consciousness level. The latter happens through spiritual quest, and practice under the guidance of a master. Goddess Saraswati depicts the awareness and wisdom that arises at this level.

It must be noted that everything related to an inner spiritual realm is depicted by everything we humans can relate to and can identify with easily – animals, husband-wife, children and so on. It is always easier to teach using what is known rather than something that is abstract. Systems that have evolved through a natural process, spanning over many generations, have this element of building their edifices from what is around. It is not the work of one grand genius that thought it all out. It just happened over eons slowly and taking its own course. Each layer of wisdom was added in an imperceptible manner in order not to disturb the human perception of the world. By doing so, the system has sustained an appeal for its citizens. One can only enter the home from the street, no matter how many alternatives he can think of. May be he can catapult himself into a home. But he still has to launch himself from the street. The street has everything, especially the streets in India – the rodents, the snakes, the pigs, the dogs, the cats, the cows, the elephants etc. along with people and vehicles. Therefore the system has evolved in such a way to include all the elements that one sees around and associates himself with. Gods appear appealing if they are presented as family members and relatives. Brahma is married to Saraswati. That is a simple enough relationship that even a child can understand and accept. At the street level one is not concerned about whether God exists or not. A child does not care if Santa Claus really exists. It is the joy of innocence that matters for the next step.

Saraswati is shown as seated on a white lotus. Lotus symbolizes non-attachment. It grows in muddy water. Yet water cannot adhere to its surface. A yogi who has achieved the Brahman status through his spiritual progress and penance acquires the wisdom that is characteristic of this state and loses all bonds and attachments. He becomes dead to all family ties and worldly desires. He lives in the world and not of the world. The Divine quality is that of non-attachment. A lotus is always presented to symbolize that state. In the case of Saraswati, both the white swan and the lotus are together. White color expresses purity, free of any dirt.

The bull is associated with Lord Shiva, the deity of dissolution. However, bull symbolizes virility. Many childless Hindu mothers offer prayer to the bull, which goes by the name Nandi. Shiva is also associated with the astrological aspects of Hindu systems (Orion the Hunter). The bull refers to a particular zodiac (Taurus). The bull reflects determination. When a bull decides to charge, it does not step back. Its pursuit is single minded. Anyone wanting to experience the state of Shiva needs a single minded, unwavering determination. Shiva appears in many forms, one of which is that of an accomplished yogi. Reaching that state requires a will and determination that is depicted by the bull.

Monkeys are abundant in India. They live in the forest and also in towns, which have replaced those forests. They hop from dangling wires on to rooftops, snatch whatever is in the hands of an unwary traveler, sit comfortably at an inaccessible place and observe everything with curiosity.

In the grand epic Ramayana, Rama, the warrior hero, meets with Hanuman, a commander in a kingdom ruled by monkeys. Rama is in search of his wife Sita, who had been kidnapped by the ten-headed demon Ravana. He is helped by Hanuman, a monkey headed general who stays till the end with Rama. He is depicted as a true warrior – one who will not fight an enemy who is not armed, one who protects anyone who surrenders to him, one who can withstand all sense based temptations and one who is humble and devout.

Hanuman represents the air element. Air is something that is freely moving. Nothing can stop it. It comes in randomly and goes out. The monkey can hop and climb in every random direction. It can leap across from branch to branch, flying through the air. One cannot predict which way it would go. A monkey head on a human body simply represents the wandering mind at the human consciousness level. If the mind is held steady and determined, then it is ready to surrender the will to the Divine as shown in the picture above.

Almost every deity has an animal associated with it in the Hindu religious system. Religion, mythology and social traditions are so deeply intertwined that it is difficult to see them apart in this system. The worshippers of Shiva and Vishnu, for a long time, remained as separate cults. They vied with each other to get royal patronage. More than a thousand years ago, the Shiva followers (known as Shaivete) and the Vishnu followers (known as Vaishnavite) formed their own orders and distinct identities. They also competed against Buddhism, which had prevailed across India. With time, Buddhism began to disappear and was replaced by other cults including Shaivism and Vaishnavism. The followers of these cults remained isolated from each other for centuries. Many myths were rewritten with the prominence of one deity over the other. Today in modern India, a separate religious identity is slowly emerging that has integrated the various cults that were once distinctly separate.

8 THE DOG AND THE CROW

So far the animals mentioned have been associated with Divine auspiciousness. The dog and the crow interestingly have been associated with doom and gloom in the Hindu belief system.

Dogs rule the streets of India. Sometimes their barks at night can be unbearable. In small towns and villages, there will be dozens of dogs at the street corners, scavenging for food and howling during the nights. Local people would be kind to them, offering them left over food. Kids would sometimes pelt stones at them and laugh at the dogs running in response. Sometimes their puppies would be the darlings of the street.

Dog is known as the man's best friend. It symbolizes loyalty. People sometimes become fiercely loyal to their beliefs and faiths. This is very much a reality at the street level of spirituality. A Street dog appropriately symbolizes the fanatical loyalty people have to their faiths, beliefs and various identities. So long as a person remains identified with anything in the material world, he would not have any inclination to leave the street and enter the temple to seek spiritual progress.

Dog is an intelligent animal. It can interact with humans much more closely than any other animal. A dog has the protective instinct towards its master and his family members. It can sense fear in people. Dogs also can respond to the aura of different individuals. I have seen dogs howl during evenings and annoying everyone in the neighborhood. A couple of days later someone would die, usually an elderly person. We would be told as children that the dogs could sense death approaching much better than we humans do. Not only dogs, many other animals can sense danger or a disaster much earlier than us. They would become restless and react before an earth quake strikes.

Dog is associated with one of the forms of Shiva, known as Bhairava. In general, dogs have not been given much importance as a cow or an elephant as auspicious beings. Shiva is known to appear as a dog. As a result, food is offered to it after any ceremony. Dogs are very rarely observed in temple sculptures. No prayer is done to a deity in the form of dog, even though dogs are aplenty in India.

Dog is also looked at as the messenger of death. Its howl is sometimes associated with someone's departure. In yogic lore, a dog's breathing cycle and its shorter life span are used as examples to illustrate the importance of slow breathing. Humans are encouraged to breathe slowly and deeply like the elephant and the tortoise. These animals are known for their longevity. A dog on the other hand pants. Dog like breathing is used as one of the Pranayama techniques by yogis (Svana Pranayama). This technique is used to eliminate toxins and mucus from the lungs. If one breathed fast like a dog, his life span would be shortened.

The crow is yet another intelligent bird. Because of its dark color, it is associated with inauspiciousness. Crows represent departed souls. It is also associated with Saturn, which brings difficult times to people. Hindu temples have a separate place for the nine celestial bodies. A human like figure will represent each body. They all would be placed such that they do not face each other. Crow is depicted as the vehicle of Saturn. By feeding crows during difficult periods, Saturn's intense effect is believed to be mitigated.

Crows also depict the ancestors. In Brahmin families, the anniversary of departed elders is celebrated ritually. Food is offered to crows with the belief that the ancestors would consume the offering through them. Crows are associated with omen. Since crows are dark and can feed on carcasses, they are associated with the dead and bad omen.

9 THE TORTOISE AND THE FISH

The tortoise has some interesting qualities. It breathes very slowly. Its longevity can span around 200 years. It moves very slowly. It is amphibious, being able to live on land as well as forage underwater. When in danger, it can simply withdraw its head and legs inside its shell so deeply that no animal can penetrate the shell. Life is in no hurry.

Vaishnavite system has the avatars of Lord Vishnu. His second avatar is in the form of a turtle. Vishnu transformed himself into a turtle when a great deluge happened. This is a cyclical phenomenon where the world is destroyed by the great flood. Vishnu, in the form of a turtle, saves the world by protecting the elements necessary for the world to revive itself. This involves the Divine and Evil elements, and the noble truths about the universe.

The world itself is believed to be standing on top of a giant tortoise, supported by elephants. The world here is not the physical world that we are familiar with. This refers to life that exists in physical body – a world of mortals. Due to the longevity of the turtle, in the Indian context, it is symbolized with eternity.

Everything is relative to the human reference frame. Compared to the ordinary mortals, the tortoise seems to live forever. The five elephants represent the physical world that exists on the earthly plane. The earthly plane does not refer only to the earth. Anything that is solid and supports physical life belongs to this plane of existence. The tortoise swims in an ocean. This is the cosmic ocean of the Universe in which the eternal spirit manifests into various forms on an earthly plane of consciousness. The image describes a concept and it is left for everyone to either literally believe it and stay at the street level or realize the meaning of it and enter the abode from the street. We have been on the street for too long. It is time to enter the abode. And the tortoise is the gateway through which we are about to enter this home.

When one consciously breathes in a slow manner, his attention begins to turn inward, much like a tortoise withdrawing its head and feet inside its shell. Breathing slowly is the first step in relaxing one's mind. The tortoise symbolizes the act of going inward, away from all the noise. Just like withdrawing itself inside its shell when threatened with adversity, one can go inward and find peace and security when facing life's adverse moments. Its head and the four legs withdrawing inside the shell symbolize the withdrawal of the senses inward during deep meditation.

The Sanskrit word for tortoise is "Koorma" or "Kurma". In the Chakra/Nadi system, there is a specific spot referred to by this name. When one meditates on this spot, his mind and body will become calm and stable. One can achieve complete withdrawal according to the Yoga Sutra of Patanjali. There are yogic postures to enhance the strength of this spot, which resembles the posture of a tortoise (legs stretched on either side like a wide V, hands locking into the legs, torso fully forward and neck stretched out).

The Sanskrit word for fish is "Matsya". Interestingly there is a legend that talks about the great flood. A man named "Manu" is forewarned by the fish about the arrival of the grand deluge. He is asked to collect all the grains and members of each animal species on his boat. When the grand deluge occurs, Lord Vishnu takes the form of a giant fish and hauls the boat to safety. Matsya avatar is the first one of the nine known avatars of Vishnu. One might see some similarity between this myth and that of Noah's ark.

In another version, the four scriptures (Vedas) are taken and hidden by a demon under the ocean. Lord Vishnu takes the form of a fish to retrieve them.

One might wonder if I am describing a zoo or not, since all my description so far has been about different animals. Well, India is a land of lions, tigers, cows, snakes and elephants isn't it? Wouldn't it be appropriate to describe its religious system from that perspective? However, it must be realized that the structure of a religious system is shaped by the history, geography, ecology, climate and biology of it. That is the secret behind its ability to survive on its own through the ages, keeping the core elements intact while modifying itself on the surface. I think this is a good place to change the direction and talk a little about other elements in the environment.

10 THE HUMAN

I have talked about the lion, the cow, the elephant, snake and many other animals and how they symbolize various aspects of spiritual life. The human stands at the entrance of the abode, just getting ready to step in from the street. His feet are bare in order to stay grounded. If we have to relate to the spirit, which does not seem perceptible, we have to start somewhere. The easiest way is to start by looking at it in the human form. We are beings that cannot survive without a relative reference system. We need a street map to locate a home. The map becomes and integral part of orienting our homes. Without the street address, the home might physically be there, but one cannot locate it.

We share many aspects of living with the animals. The forces of nature bind us. We cannot survive without the sun's light, or the atmosphere, water and the earth. However, we are capable of designing our own homes and building them. We have the capability to make sound, much like all other animals. But we have taken it a step higher. We can express in a language that has a structure to it. We can take it even higher – we can sing and create music. There is a faculty in us that is really not needed to exist on this earth. We could live just like all the other animals, relying on nature to provide us or perish when the conditions turn adverse. But we have this extra capability that has spawned creativity in many aspects. We have languages, music, literature, art, science and technology. We are always eager to know what is beyond the world we know. If our goal is simply to survive and exist, we could have used our extra faculty to do just that. But we have not stopped with that. We have discovered many things through indirect means and logical deductions. We have begun to look at the universe around us. We are able to predict the existence of exotic objects and using the process of indirect observation, we are able to confirm their existence. Modern scientific world has made great strides looking outward and reaching things that are far beyond our senses and capabilities.

Centuries ago, the Indian sages took the same task and began to explore the universe from a different approach – by going inwards. In that process, they discovered the grand truth of interconnectedness between everything in the universe. The emphasis shifted towards not defining anything or explaining about everything. Everything is as it is. Therefore the interest became focused on experiencing what is and simply describing it in terms of our observational capabilities. This brought images, deities, Gods, mythology, epics, scriptures and philosophy. They realized way early that one can never make another individual really know something about his inner experience. It can only be understood if the other individual experiences the same thing and can now acknowledge it. We all experience life through the processes of breathing, consuming, reproducing, up bringing and being aware. We all know what a headache is. No one can describe it exactly. Yet we all can understand the experience of it. The sages in India realized that the inward journey of spiritual experience could only be understood by experiencing it. One can try to describe it in various ways. But explanations are going to be incomplete and interpretations can multiply. When Buddha was asked about God, he maintained silence. He knew what it meant and the only way to know about it is through inner experience. God is just a word denoting that inner experience. It only points to something and does not become what is being denoted.

The Hindu system evolved in such a way to let people explore various options available to them, in various ways that appeals to them and accommodate the nature of the different individuals. Everyone is unique in some way. No two people perceive anything around the same way. The inner experience varies from person to person. What appeals to one individual may appall some other individual. We all have our own tendencies and preferences. Our maturity levels vary. Our experiences differ. In such a situation, the best way to provide any spiritual guidance is to make it simple at the outset. The starting point always has to be simple, relevant and be on terms that we can relate to.

If we were to teach complex algebra to first graders, we know it is impossible. They are not ready for it. They need to go through the steps of learning the necessary basics and grow mature at the same time, in order to be ready to learn a complex mathematical subject. At the first grade level, teaching takes a very different shape. Things are taught in a way children can relate to according to their perception of the world. In that world, Disney characters are real. Santa Claus is real. The little mermaid is real. Animals talk and behave just like us humans. Everything is one giant playing room. Everything is a toy to be played with. There are no concerns about the future or what is ahead in life. They wonder why they have to learn things that make no sense. They have no idea what rules are. They have to be taught good manners. Teaching young children is one of the most difficult tasks. The only way they can learn is through playing. They love to sing. They like cutting and pasting things. They are eager to mess their hands with clay and sand. They like to jump and slide. They need a lot of recess period and stickers. Teaching is done through a process that a child can relate to. Understanding will happen on its own, at a latter time.

The Hindu religious system has adopted the same approach. Humans may be growing into adults. Yet from a spiritual standpoint, they are much like first grade children. They like the street much more than the home where discipline is needed. The street is free. One can run everywhere, scream at the top of the voice and watch everything that is going on – marches, festivals and fun activities. At home, one encounters rules and spiritual children do not like it. They like to explore to the inner spiritual world in a way they can relate to.

It is not that some genius sat somewhere and designed the whole thing out. It never happens in a natural process. Evolution is an accepted fact in science. It seems incredible to even think about how complex we humans are and how all these things happened, by the simple process of evolution. We cannot help leaning our thoughts towards a grand human being who designed it all. Then comes the question of who designed that grand human. Evolution does not bother about addressing anyone's design or plans. It is a process and everything simply happens in that process. The same kind of evolution has happened in the case of Hindu religious systems. What is natural always sticks and survives. Even if something artificial is imposed on it, it will begin to penetrate through it and consume it at some point in time. Natural tendencies are not easy to contain.

Any system that evolves by recognizing the natural tendencies and uses them as steps towards spiritual progress has managed to survive. It appeals to people. When times change, so do the tendencies. And the system shifts accordingly without anyone really controlling it. It is a very slow and imperceptible process. Most people at the street level know that whatever has been set up is mostly symbolic in nature. Only many do not know how they work. And no one is sweating about it. Understanding will happen as one makes a progress. And progress always happens for one amongst many. Such a process is called nucleation. Ice forms by nucleating in freezing water at various points and then growth spreads in all directions. Growth happens so long as conditions remain favorable and the rates vary as a result. The growing facets meet at their boundaries resulting in a multitude of ice sheets. Nucleation and growth is a natural process. Everything in nature happens by this process. Various factors and conditions decide where nucleation happens. The Hindu systems have followed this nucleation and growth process through ages.

Religions have been needed to fulfill the spiritual thirst in humans. They have helped people observe codes of conduct according to societal needs. They have helped people live together and be harmonious. Religions are the first grade curricula for spiritual progress in humans. They have a lot of simplistic elements that prevail mostly at the street level. As a result, very few seek to step out of the street and enter the inner realm of their homes. Many stay at the first grade level on spiritual terms. And that is perfectly all right and normal.

We see life in all forms around us. The multitude of beings is mind-boggling. Everyone is living a life and we wonder what the purpose is. Why is everyone being born, struggles to live and then die away? A hundred years from now, no one will know who you are, unless you made a mark for yourself in history. A billion years from now, that history itself might disappear and no one will care. So why are we coming and going? What is the purpose of all kinds of vegetation, animals and humans to exist? Do we care about someone else' sorrow? If someone had a miserable life a thousand years ago, does that affect us much? What is the purpose of all emotions? Well, the answer is simple. There is no purpose. Things come into existence and go. A few billion years from now, scientists have forecast about the demise of this planet itself. The sun will expand and its surface would be so close to our planet that it can get pulled into the sun. Much before that the oceans and atmosphere would be burnt off. Nothing as we know now will exist then. What a waste isn't it? Would someone feel bad about it? All this billions of years of organic life that evolved into complex forms and some of them developed incredible awareness would have disappeared without a trace. So where does it all come from and where does it go? One cannot find those answers at the street level. And the purpose is not to find such an answer itself. We exist now and why not make the most of it and be done with it? We did not exist a billion years ago. And that does not worry us. How does it matter if we do not exist a billion years from now?

According to the Hindu belief system, we always exist – as consciousness. Sometimes it manifests in a physical form or any other form that we do not know about or can perceive. Sometimes it does not. Therefore what is important is the consciousness. One has to use this word because there is no other word available. Words are limited expressions of an experience or an event or a process. Expressions are not important – Experience is. One can experience something if he or she is conscious of it. Take the breath for example. Most of us simply breathe, not paying much attention to it. But the consciousness of it can become extremely acute if we were to lose the breath. If someone is stuck inside a billowing smoke or is deep underwater drowning, breath becomes precious. Such near death experiences reveal the preciousness of everything we do not pay much attention to. Breath is life. Paying attention to it brings the conscious experience of it. It makes that experience inward. That is the entrance to the home from the street.

Most stay at the street level and disappear. Very few have the desire to enter the home and find themselves. As they enter, they begin to understand the various things on the street and their purpose. This understanding also varies between individuals. There is still a long way to go towards the inner sanctum. So the religious system suddenly shifts itself to give a different perspective as one enters the next grade in spiritual education.

A religious system has many aspects to it. Everything is not associated with the temple and its rituals. There are social aspects that include traditional practices, festivals and events. Everything is tied in somehow. Astrology is a very important aspect of the whole system. Everything is decided based on astrological calculations. When astrology in involved, the realization that we are not as independent as we think emerges.

11 COSMIC CONNECTIVITY

The general belief in the Hindu astrological system is that every human is directly connected to the universe. There are aspects in the human body and mind that correspond to cosmological bodies and phenomena. Therefore, our minds and actions can be influenced by the cosmos. In order to be aware and negotiate our ways through everyday life, one relies on astrology. This is similar to the advanced GPS systems we have in modern cars where it can determine if there is a traffic jam somewhere on the road and provide an alternative route on its own. In the astrological belief viewpoint, there are different possibilities one can go through under a given set of circumstances. If one is aware of those possibilities and chose the correct one, then life could go on with minimal setbacks.

It must be remembered here that I am only providing a description and not an argument for or against this ancient system. My goal here is to educate the reader about what is out there and how it works. Many people today wash astrology off as hocus-pocus. Astrology is being ignored because there are too many quacks making wrongful predictions about the future and the modern world has changed its attitude towards it. However, astrology plays a very big part in the socio-religious lives of Hindus. When a child is born, its horoscope is constructed. The date and time of the birth are carefully recorded and demanded by the relatives. Everyone is curious to know what the child will turn out to be.

We know that celestial bodies affect our daily lives. We cannot exist without the sun. Its energy gives us sustenance. It drives the weather on this planet and the seasons. Its energy is converted into food by plants, which are consumed by us. The moon affects the tides. There is the circadian rhythm where life has evolved around lunar cycles. Menstrual period and ovulation in women correspond to the lunar cycles. The full moon induces romantic feelings. The mentally unstable one is called as a lunatic. Moon seems to affect our minds, may be because of its proximity to the earth and its gravitational interaction. Other celestial bodies might be quite far from the earth and their influence may not be much when thought of intuitively. However, the astrological system includes many celestial bodies, their movements, the constellations and stars to create charts based on calculations. One may not see much from a physical effect standpoint. However, from a mind-spirit standpoint, the influence and interactions of the celestial bodies are considered significant in Hindu astrology.

The Hindu astrological system relies on the positions of certain stars instead of the movement of the sun and the moon. It is called the Sidereal system. Since relative to the earth, the stars are so far away that they appear stationary, it makes it a lot easier to chart everything on a horoscope according to the stars. There are 27 such stars that are included for constructing the horoscopes and calendars. Also the calendar system is lunar and not solar. Birthday celebrations, marriage anniversaries etc. are decided based on the lunar calendar and the stars. As a result, one will find their anniversary dates not matching exactly with the Gregorian calendar system.

Festivals and religious rituals are fixed based on the sidereal astrological calculations. The zodiacs are similar to the Greek system. There are 12 zodiacs. However, they are reversed with respect to the Greek system because the Indian sub-continent is sub-tropical and falls on the southern side of the hemisphere. For example, the Hindu Zodiac sign Aquarius will correspond to the Greek Zodiac Leo. Months vary in number of days, as the calendar system is lunar. The waxing (Krishna) and waning (Shukla) cycles of the moon and the eclipses are extremely important in the system.

The zodiacs correspond to centers in the human body. For example, Aries corresponds to the head, Taurus to the neck and chest and so on. Scorpio corresponds to reproductive organs. Similarly celestial objects have their corresponding centers in the body – the sun and the moon for example.

The human body is not just a physical entity alone. There are five layers, or sheaths, of which only the physical body is visible to the sensory organs that deal with vision, hearing, smell, taste and touch. It is the four other layers that have the cosmological connections, linking us to the universe. The five layers are known as "Koshas". The five sheaths appear like Russian dolls, each one inside the other. First is the physical body that we are all familiar with (Annamaya Kosha). This is surrounded by the body of life force or Prana (Pranamaya Kosha). Then comes the mental and emotional body (Manomaya Kosha). The body of wisdom is the next one (Vigyanamaya Kosha). The final sheath is made up of bliss (Anandamaya Kosha). According to this view, the mind is not confined to the brain. The brain is only the physical component that operates at that level and mind and emotions operate through the brain from the mental sheath. The same goes for memories stored. One cannot physically sense these sheaths, much like we cannot see the mind and memory if we cut up the brain of a dead person. All we would see are the physical components of it. Using electrical signals, we can sense what is going on in the brain during a mind activity, but cannot literally tell what it is.

The physical body thus becomes a temporary vehicle into which the universal consciousness enters at a chosen astrological time and location, and exists for a time period, experiences life as predicted in the horoscope. Not only one's life process, but also the nature of the individual is predictable according to this system. The nature does not arise from genetics. Rather it resides in the other four layers and when the time is right, an appropriate family is found in which the being is born with that nature that seems to fit the lineage of the family. This is the view of the system. One's life fortunes and miseries have been set up even before being born in the physical body. Anything that enters a body from the cosmic realm undergoes the same human experience of life and struggle. Struggles are there mainly to create the awareness. Until awareness happens, the cycle of birth, death and rebirth continue. Astrology and reincarnation of a being are deeply entrenched in the Hindu belief system. No matter how many religions and cults are there in the system, the belief in reincarnation and gaining awareness through life's experience forms important elements of the system.

When a person dies, the physical body (Sthoola Sharira) is abandoned. The other layers of the sheath remain, keeping all memories and records. These sheaths are collectively termed as the Astral body (Sukshma Sharira). Cosmological connectivity occurs through the astral body. Physical activities like breathing are directly linked to the astral activities. In the sheath of the life force, Prana enters and exits in coordination with our physical breath cycle. By gaining control over the breath through various breathing exercises known as Pranayama, one can gain control and access to the life-force sheath. A physical body is said to be alive so long as the Prana is circulating in the Pranamaya sheath.

Through the practice of Pranayama and Yoga one is able to achieve a synchronization of the physical and pranic layers with the mental layer. This helps achieve mind control and concentration that facilitates meditation. However, blockages are present that prevent this connectivity between the different layers from happening. These blockages happen due to various reasons, including one's actions and choices. They are cumulatively built up over one's life time as well as previous life times. Until the blockages are cleared, one is unable to make spiritual progress and his perception of the world around becomes limited and primitive. Blockages can be dissolved in many ways – through selfless service to others, through chanting of mantras, going on pilgrimages and offering prayers, observing fast and penance, abstaining from certain habits and through the practice of Pranayama and Yoga. This is the reason why many activities are followed in the Hindu systems. If the blockages remain, they begin to change one's tendencies and nature. The more the blockage, the more clouded a person becomes. His spiritual energy is suppressed

and he becomes more like an animal, relying on the senses and instincts with limited awareness about the world around himself.

One tends to prefer the street to the home from a spiritual standpoint.

12 CAUSE AND EFFECT

I talked about blockages in the ethereal sheaths that inhibit a person from becoming aware of the universe within him. These blockages are a result of one's conscious choices and actions. They happen through the process of Karma. Every action has a cause and an effect. Each action is also made from a choice at every instant. Any outward action causes Karma. This means for each action there is a payback. The payback can be beneficial or detrimental. Actions are happening all the time because we interact with other beings in this world. What we do, affects others in some way. Whether an action is something said or done, it has an impact. Even a thought has an impact. If we affected others negatively in any way, at some point in life or in some other life, that action will be compensated for, by us experiencing the same thing from someone else or the being that was affected by us. This process of compensation occurs naturally to help us remove the blockage that has built up. Karma is there to clear the blockages to spiritual progress if we so desire to pursue it. Unless we clear the blockage and repay the karmic debt, our desires to make spiritual progress would face hindrance. Karma is a major aspect of the Hindu belief systems. Suffering and recovery from it are the main principles of Buddhism as well.

Even though we do not like to suffer, suffering is a relative term. One cannot draw it on an absolute scale. A person born with visual impairment can accept a life without vision and is really not suffering from it. A person born in a place where he has to walk many miles to fetch food and water does not really suffer from it as everyone else around is doing the same. However, if one were to lose vision due to an accident, that experience of not having vision anymore can be deeply profound. If a person is used to having 24 hour guarantee of water and other amenities suddenly finds himself in a desolate place where he has to walk for miles to get his basic needs met, he will suffer. A rich man might find it hard to sleep on a stone bench after losing all his wealth. A poor man who never knew how a mattress feels can comfortably sleep on a stone bench. Thus suffering becomes internal and it depends upon what one really misses. There is physical suffering and mental one. It is the latter that affects people the most. Physical suffering is accepted. If one is hurt physically due to illness or an accident, at some point it is accepted and life goes on. But if one is affected mentally, it just doesn't go away. It keeps coming back and piles on top of all other issues in one's memory. People suffer from stress, tension, fears, grief and these create blockages in the energy channels of the astral body. And they are a result of one's karma.

***

Long ago, there lived a small businessman somewhere in India. He was in his sixties and life had been one miserable experience to him. He took over a business that was running successfully when his father ran it and somehow, under his management, the business had been teetering on the edge. His investments did not yield the expected profits and debt burden increased. He spent sleepless nights, worried about losing everything. He could not think of just giving it up. His survival depended on it. Somehow he seemed to miss the luck that everyone else had. People who ventured into business after him had become quite successful and rich. Every decision he had taken had turned for the worst. He cursed his fate all the time. His son grew up irresponsibly, lacking any skill or worry about his own future career. His wife never trusted him or his abilities. He hated coming home. As time went on, he found things to get worse than better. He sought a way out of it. He had been waiting for his lucky break that seemed to evade him.

Someone told him about a healer in the nearby town who could take away the miseries in people using his magical powers. Having tried everything else, the businessman found this prospect to be attractive. Nothing else had worked. Why not try magic? So he went to meet the healer. The healer's home was crowded. The businessman had to wait for his turn. It took him a few days of patient waiting to get the invitation to enter the healing room. The healer looked at the businessman and smiled.

"What brings you here?" asked the healer.

The businessman wondered if he was being cheated or not. If this man were a powerful healer, wouldn't he know everything intuitively? Did one have to spell out his problem to him? Everyone came there to resolve his problem and not for a chat. But one had to be polite because the healer was not the person in need.

"I am a businessman. I am in my sixties. Everything that I have attempted has been a failure. My debt burden is increasing. My business is collapsing. No one likes me. Everyone ill-treats me. I have no respect. I am having a miserable time. I need help from you to make all these miseries go away"

The healer was full of smile when the businessman was narrating his problems. He did not seem to be in any hurry. He sat in silence for sometime. Then he sighed. The businessman wondered what he was up to.

"Well, I will heal you for sure. Your miseries will go away. But you need to know the causes for your misery first"

"And how will I find the causes?"

The healer was quiet for sometime. Then he mentioned the name of a town where the businessman had to go and meet a person. He mentioned the name of this person and said that the businessman had to meet him before returning. Without meeting him, he could not hope to find any healing.

The businessman wondered where this town was. This was the 1800s. One did not have maps and modern facilities. By asking around, he realized that this town was somewhere quite far from where he lived. It was on the other side of a mountain range that one could see along the horizon from his town. He decided to go to that place and meet this man. He was curious about why he had to meet him and what the healer was going to do with the outcome of that meeting.

He told his family he would be gone for a few days on business and left on his bullock cart. It took him two weeks of hard travel to go over the rough roads and take the treacherous path on the mountains, facing rain and wind and finally reach this town that the healer had mentioned. As soon as he entered he started asking about this man the healer wanted him to meet. No one seemed to know someone by that name in that town. In those days, communities were small and everyone knew everyone else around. It seemed strange that no one knew this man the businessman was looking for. When people asked for a description of the man, the businessman only had a name. They wondered why someone had to travel from that far with no information about someone he was trying to meet. Days went by. It was getting to be a frustrating experience. The businessman wondered if he had gone to the wrong town or not. He inquired about towns with the same name and everyone said that there was no other town with that name. Only no one seemed to know the person he was looking for.

Dejected, the businessman gave up and decided to return. He was vexed at the healer for making him waste his time and resources like this. He cursed his fate again. The healer too made his life miserable. He got ready to leave. In those days, the local residents gave travelers food and shelter. It was a custom to welcome travelers and host them. The businessman was offered his morning meal at the last house on the street before his departure. He was invited to come inside and have his meal served. As he was eating, the businessman saw an old woman at the corner staring at him. She was extremely senile. But she seemed to look at him with some anger. Suddenly she started cursing him and yelling at him. The host apologized for this inconvenience.

"I am sorry. This is my mother. She has lost her mind. For the past few years she has been yelling and screaming for no reason. She has no idea where she is. Her memory is fading. Hope you will understand"

The businessman did not mind. He felt no one really liked him. Therefore it was normal for someone to scream at him for no reason. Such was his luck. He was taken by surprise when the old woman started cursing about someone suddenly. The name she mentioned was interesting. It was the name he had been asking everyone about. Until then no one had any recognition of it.

"Excuse me, does your mother know this person?" the businessman was curious to find out.

"Let me ask," the host replied. With great difficulty, the host managed to make his mother talk about the person whose name the businessman was interested about.

"Oh that moron! Who wants to know about him?" She spat. "The greedy, wily, clever egomaniac! Who would want to associate himself with him? Even rotten street dogs will hate his sight" She went on a harangue that was unbearable. "Whoever this man was," the businessman thought, "must have been a terrible man"

"Can your mother tell us where I can find this man?" he asked quietly.

"Who wants to meet him? We are so happy he died long ago. We celebrated big time when he died finally. That monster," she went on further. The businessman learned that this person died many decades ago when the woman was quite young. He was a powerful man in that town and basically leached everyone to get wealthy and no one liked him as a result. But they could do nothing about it. All they could do was to curse him and he was too powerful for anyone to go after him. They waited it out and the man died one day, bringing relief and joy to everyone in the town. Many years went by and those who knew him died away one by one, having been replaced by a newer generation that seemed to have forgotten about him. The town had moved on. This woman was one of those who lived during the terrible times the previous generation experienced under this man.

The businessman wondered why the healer would want him to go and meet someone who had been dead decades ago? It was close to seventy years since that man died. He was convinced that the healer was having fun at his expense. He was going to return and teach that healer a lesson he could not forget.

He returned to his hometown after a couple of weeks and did not wait for anything. He went straight to the healer's house. He pushed aside everyone and walked right into his room.

"Oh you are back! Well, tell me about what you saw?"

The man was about to pounce on the healer. But there were others around.

"You were supposed to heal me. Instead you made my life even more miserable by making me go to some unknown place, search for someone who had been dead seventy years ago and whom everyone hated. What are you trying to achieve by all this?"

"Seventy years ago? That's what I thought," said the healer.

"What are you saying?"

"Let me see. How old are you now?"

"Why? I am sixty five"

"Hmm. That makes sense," said the holy man smiling at the businessman.

Suddenly the businessman sensed something. Was he saying that his miseries in this life are a result of his past life? Did the healer send him to meet his own past incarnation?

The healer gave him a teasing look.

The businessman smiled. He simply walked out. He understood what the healer had done. It took him an entire lifetime to realize what he had been through and the reason for it. His miserable experience pushed him to find a way out and that pursuit took him to a realization that he had caused all that pain to himself. All this suffering would not have resulted if he had been a good man in the past. Instead of being cursed by everyone, he could have been thanked or praised. He realized that no one gets away with anything he does. He became peaceful after that. Life's miseries no longer affected him. He was paying his debt and he thanked the Gods for letting him pay it off in his current life.

***

No one is exempt from the effect of Karma, not even the Gods. There is the story of the warrior prince Rama in the epic Ramayana where he hides and kills a man named Vali in order to help his brother Shugreev get the kingdom. The two appear identical. And Shugreev is the weaker of the two. He keeps losing to Vali in every combat and seeks Rama's help. Rama needs the help of Shugreev's army to find his missing wife Sita. He tells Shugreev to wear a garland the next time he gets into a combat with his brother. When Vali and Shugreev fight, Rama is able to tell the difference and shoots Vali down with his arrow. Vali realizes what had happened. As he is dying he asks Rama why he hid himself despite being a great warrior. Rama is the human incarnation of Lord Vishnu. This action by Rama sets up the debt of Karma. It is not paid in that lifetime. Later on, in another life, Vishnu reincarnates as Krishna.

In the second great epic of India, the Mahabharata, towards the end of the story, Krishna is lying down resting. A hunter appears looking for his prey. As he shoots his arrow, it pierces Krishna's foot. The hunter realizes what he has done, but he could not help Krishna who is dying of bleeding. Krishna knows what the underlying reason for this end is. He does not prevent it and allows his mortal body to go through to its end. The hunter in this life was Vali in the past life. Thus even God enters the field of karma when taking a human form.

Most beings on this plane of existence have come to cleanse

themselves by paying off their Karma. It is difficult to prove whether Karma is real or if it is a religious belief. Sometimes karma is paid off collectively. Various beings with similar karma arrive and suffer through at the same time. One has to look at history to draw inferences. To me, the suffering of the Russians and Eastern Europeans under close to 70 years of Communist rule was like collective karma. They were all under the grip of the Soviet Union, which was a mighty super power on its own. No one could have imagined its disappearance suddenly into thin air. When the wall was broken in Berlin, history was made. New countries emerged. Old gave way for the new. No one could force this using military might. With all its nuclear weapons and missiles, the Soviet Union simply collapsed and disappeared, bringing freedom to millions of people. Many perished under the Soviet rule much before that under dictators like Stalin. The new Arab Spring is yet another phase in history where events happen all of a sudden having a tremendous impact on the world. The collapse and disappearance of the mighty British Empire is another example. When changes are destined, they happen no matter what the odds are. Prior to that, any attempt to change the status does not succeed. Everything happens on its own time.

Suffering is an integral part of inner cleansing. One, who is ready to receive an inner spiritual progress, sees suffering as a stepping-stone. Until then, one ends up carrying it on his back. If a sailor saw only smooth seas, he will have very little experience. Only a rough sea makes a good sailor. Suffering is needed to learn. Karma is like physical pain. Pain is there to protect us from over exerting damaged parts in our bodies. It acts like a warning alarm signal until healing happens. Karma is there to bring us back to our pure state by acting as a trigger for awareness. If one suffers without knowing why, that suffering ultimately will drive him to seek a solution and the root cause of it. Once he realizes both, he is bound to protect himself from repeating the choice that led to that suffering. That is the function of Karma. People have to undergo the drama of life to learn from it. Values are realized from within through direct experience. In such a drama, conflicts arise and good and evil appear. Even at the Demigod level, there are good and evil beings in the Hindu system.

Those on the good side become known as Devas and those on the other side are Asuras. Devas and Asuras are elevated beings. They have developed spiritual powers. Yet one group turns evil compared to the other. In the tug of war between the two, the drama of life unfolds. Through the drama, experience arises and through experience revelation happens. This is depicted as the churning of the elixir of immortality. The Devas and Asuras churn the cosmic ocean for the elixir of immortality. They use a giant snake named Vasuki for this purpose.

This churning brought in Lords Shiva and Vishnu and all the Devas and Asuras. Through the churning of the cosmic ocean many gifts appeared, along with poison. Lord Shiva was requested to help and He consumed the poison. His consort Parvati held his neck so that the poison does not spread across his body, the Universe. As a result, Shiva has a blue colored neck where poison is held. Interestingly, blue is a color representing the throat Chakra. Ancient mythologies gave a human dimension to the Gods, who fought wars, romanced, were cursed, suffered, betrayed, won and enjoyed life, just like we humans do. The children in us always understand when we can relate to anything on our own human terms.

In reality, the two sides – Devas and Asuras exist within each one of us. We have the choice at each instant and depending upon the choices we make, the outcome varies. The outcome in turn decides what kind of choices we would face further on. Our senses and emotions are needed to enter the spiritual realm. Both positive and negative qualities need to be integrated. This integration initially resembles a churning action. The poison that first emerges symbolizes the tests one will face when undertaking spiritual quest. One has to go past the test in order to continue the ascent. The extremes (Devas and Asuras) work together to extract the elixir of immortality, which is the Universal spirit. The coming together of extremes and their integration is important in one's spiritual journey. The mind is represented by the mountain (steady) and is not affected by the churning forces. It is supported at the bottom by a giant tortoise, which represents the withdrawal of senses and intense focus. The snake represents living in the body to attain spiritual immortality. The ocean is made of milk, which symbolizes the Universe.

The Hindu mythology was not confined to Gods and Demigods alone. Humans took active part in them. These varied from ordinary people to great sages and seers. The entire epic of Mahabharata is one single poem. In fact it is the world's longest poem. The story on it goes like this. There was a sage named Vyasa. He compiled the epic of Mahabharata. He wanted to dictate the whole thing while in meditation. No ordinary mortal could keep up with the rendering. Therefore Lord Ganesh was approached. Lord Ganesh promised write it all down. But there was one issue. Lord Ganesh does not stop, once he starts. That means, Vyasa had to continuously recite without any pause. Vyasa made a clever scheme. He requested that Lord Ganesh write only if he could understand everything he was writing. The Lord agreed. Vyasa would recite the poem. In between, he would make complicated phrases that would make Lord Ganesh pause in order to understand. Vyasa used that time to compose more. So goes the story.

There is a hidden meaning here. Think of your breath. As soon as one emerges from the womb, breath cycles start. And they continue until a state when we say that a person has breathed his last. Breath does not stop. It continues from the beginning, all the way to the end. It can be paused or slowed down sometimes at will. But it cannot be stopped for too long by ordinary mortals. Lord Ganesh's writing refers to our breath. The whole epic of Mahabharata narrates a war between brothers and their relatives. But the underlying meaning refers to our own individual selves. That is why breath is very important. Our stories are written with our breaths. They happen so long as we live and we live until we breathe our last.

In order to understand the hidden meaning of the epics and other myths, we have to develop knowledge about the real spiritual system that is not easily visible from the street level. We are ready to enter the abode now and understand the Chakras and Nadis.

13 THE SPIRITUAL BODY

Our general perception of the world around is limited to our five senses – vision, hearing, smell, taste and touch. We share this world with other beings, which also rely on these senses. They differ from each other based on which one of the senses they rely more than the others. Our sense of smell is not as acute as that of a canine. Our sense of hearing is not as sharp as that of an owl. Our vision is not as powerful as that of a cat in terms of light sensing or that of an eagle when it comes to distant resolution. We cannot sense certain color variations that certain insects can detect. We simply lack remote sensing that a snake uses in detecting heat. We exist within our realm based on our needs. However, we have one aspect that is unique in this world – awareness. We have a much better awareness of the world around us and that has helped us survive better under extremely varying conditions without having to naturally adapt much. We use tools and other means to protect ourselves. Though we are part of the animal world, something sets us apart. We are dominating this world as a result. The entire animal kingdom seems to be aware of this fact.

On this earthly plane, we seem to be enjoying a supreme position of dominance. And there is a vast variation amongst us ranging from animal like existence to almost Divine like qualities. We cannot sense anything beyond what our five senses can tell us. The question is this – are there senses beyond smell, taste, vision, touch and hearing? I can mention about intuition. Some people have extremely acute level of intuition. Is there anything beyond intuition? Is the Universe the way we perceive it or is its true dimension very different? If a cow were to see the road, its vision is vastly different from that of ours. Cows are colorblind and lack an ability to judge depth. We are gifted with binocular vision which helps us judge correctly the distance of an object from us and whether it is moving away from us or coming towards us. Every animal has evolved differently according to its own needs. As a result, the perception of reality can vary vastly based on what the evolution behind that perception is. Some animals can sense what we cannot and we can sense certain things animals cannot. And it is possible both our animal friends and us may not be sensing things that are out there. It is just that our evolution has not found the need for them.

We have the capability to look inward with awareness. There is a feeling that we are somehow connected to the Universe around us. However we cannot tell how. Those who have succeeded in knowing this connectivity have mentioned about the spiritual body, Chakras and Nadis. These go by different names and references in other parts of the world. It is not a strict monopoly of India. Human beings can experience the same thing in any part of the world and they have given these different names. When I describe about these spiritual aspects, someone from a different culture might recognize certain similarities.

The field of Indian Astrology is rooted in the belief that the Universe does affect each individual through a cosmic interaction. This interaction happens through the process of Karma. The position of the celestial bodies relative to the place and time of physical birth seems to be unique for each individual. That uniqueness arises due to individual karma. This means each being dissolves and emerges back and forth like a wave in the cosmic ocean. We call the dissolution process the death of the physical body and the emergence as the birth in a new body. Every individual reincarnates until all cleansing of blockages happens. The desire to cleanse arises due to suffering through the drama of life. Without suffering, one simply will not realize the need to purge the blockages. We do not like to suffer from pain. But pain has a purpose. It protects us from hurting ourselves more. If pain sensation did not exist, we would be running around with torn muscles and ligaments and broken bones. Pain sets up a limit on our hurt body parts from being used until healing happens. Suffering in life is very similar. It triggers the desire to find ways out of it. In the process, one discovers the path.

Buddha called it the eight-fold path. Buddhism simply negated all the social aspects of the Hindu religions and began to focus directly on the spiritual aspects. The need to start from the street level was not considered as important. On the spiritual front, Buddhism shares a lot of aspects with the Hindu systems. In order to cleanse the blockages to spiritual progress, Buddhism advocated selfless service to fellow humans and animals. In addition, its monastic tradition propagated the spiritual aspects of meditation, Chakras and Nadis across most of Asia. These spiritual elements are popular in the world today because of Buddhism's reach. However, these elements are an integral part of the Hindu religious system itself and predate Buddhism.

If one looked at the Hindu temples, rituals, traditions, myths and epics they are all based on the Chakras, Nadis and spiritual bodies. The only difference between the Hindu religions and Buddhism is that there has been a deliberate effort to keep them away from the street level in the latter. It is possible because humans can turn into Asuras. There are many stories that depict such humans who started out on a sincere way and ended up as monsters. The Divine had to put an end to their powers. Abuse of spiritual powers can happen when ego is the driving force. The caste system in India began to get entrenched due to the abuse of spiritual powers. Buddha left that system and preached something differently because he stood up against the idea of privilege by one's birth. There is always the danger of a system going out of control and turning monstrous. We saw this happen in Nazi Germany where a population that grew in an advanced, and industrialized nation, turned into a warped ideological state and the world had to go to war with it to end it.

As one ascends spiritually, clearing the karmic blockages, there is always the danger of the fall. Anyone at any time can be defeated by desires, power and ego and fall hard. The game of snakes and ladders symbolizes this truth. The more one tries to cleanse himself in order to progress spiritually, the more he is tested by life's circumstances. The higher one's spiritual level, the more is the weight of the karma for every action and the harder is the fall. The Indian subcontinent is said to have suffered from this collective Karma for more than a thousand years when its temples were razed, towns and villages were plundered, people taken as slaves and ruled by outsiders with alien religions. The Karma of abuse brought that debt on its people and they had to pay for it over generations. In order to prevent further abuse, the whole advanced spiritual practice has remained rather esoteric and hidden. One who seeks is severely tested before being accepted. The rest are left to live an ordinary life at the street level. Thus the Hindu systems have two distinct sides to them – one that is mostly at the first grade level and one that has advanced to the PhD level. The latter is a small minority. But they have preserved the spirit of it over centuries.

The spiritual body is made up of four sheaths surrounding the physical body. This is something I had mentioned earlier. The spiritual body is also referred to as the ethereal body or the astral body. Until Karmic blocks are cleansed, the astral body exists at an individual level, reincarnating in newer physical bodies. Once all karmic blocks are purged, there is a choice to merge with the Universe. Or one can choose to remain at a spiritual level to help other seekers purge their karmic blockages. Thus goes the belief system.

In the spiritual body lie the equivalent of our physical nerves. These are termed as Nadis. Life force flows through the Nadis. The flow of life force or Prana is synchronized with our physical breaths. We store our emotions and memories in the Astral body. And they begin to restrict the flow of prana. The Indian spiritual masters have named the various Nadis in the astral body. According to them, there are 72000 Nadis in a human astral body. Some of the Nadis bear the same name as celestial elements as well as rivers, animals and mountains.

In a spiritually elevated person, the presence of these Nadis is sensed. Those who had made tremendous advancement in spiritual progress have developed the whole map of the Nadis. Nadis intersect at various places and form nodes. The locations of these nodes appear like vortices or whirling circles known as Chakras. There are 108 Chakras in a spiritual body. Of these 7 are considered as primary for spiritual elevation. They are located along the back of the spine. There are hundreds of books and material available that describe the Chakra-Nadi system in extremely vivid details. I will cover as much needed on how the Hindu religious system has placed all its aspects around the Chakra-Nadi structure. The science of Tantra has the most detailed knowledge developed on the Chakra-Nadi system.

14 TANTRA - FROM PHYSICAL TO BEYOND PHYSICAL

The word Tantra (pronounced as "Tha","n", and "thrA". The letter "n" is not accentuated) has become symbolic of exotic sex in today's world. There are many books that deal with enhancing sexual joy by using Tantric postures. The important thing about Tantra is that it uses two aspects – the male and the female. The coming together of the male and the female is used in enhancing spiritual energy's passage through the practitioners under the guidance of an adept. However, modern world has stamped Tantra to have a specific meaning of enhancing sensual pleasure.

The ancient Hindu systems do not consider sex as a sinful act. Sexual union is considered Divine because that act leads to creation of another human being. People forget the fact that sex involves not just the physical act of sense pleasure alone. It involves the flow of love and affection between two individuals and brings them closer each time. That process triggers vibrations that help enhance the spirit inside each person, which leads to a harmonious relationship. A picture cannot depict that experience. Sexual union will result in a vibratory resonance of the sacral and heart Chakras when love and affection flow. If only the sacral Chakra is involved, people tend to gravitate more towards the animal side of existence. Tantric practice of sexual union is meant to open up the Nadis in both the male and the female to provide a pathway for the flow of Divine energy in order to experience the union. The yogis who engage in Tantric sex also practice absorbing everything through their sexual organs rather than release anything. There are special yogic practices to enhance the absorption. This helps absorb the energy that is liberated from both the male and the female. One must have a mindset that is completely devoid of any vulgarity to engage in real Tantric sexual union. It is not for ordinary mortals who view the world from the streets.

The belief in Tantric sex is that spiritual energy is more in the female than in the male. The sexual practice is called "Maithuna", where ejaculation is blocked and the energy of the orgasm is directed upward through the central Nadi named Sushumna to the crown spot above one's head.

Tantra is about balance. Inside each human being, be it a male or female, there are masculine and feminine aspects. There is no mortal who is a perfect male or the perfect female, until one can achieve the state of immortality through self-realization. True masculine aspects include courage, strength, calmness, ability to choose wisely, protecting those who surrender, standing up against temptations and being protective. True feminine aspects include unconditional love, compassion, empathy, surrender and forgiveness. The masculine aspects tend to belong to the lower three chakras, while the feminine aspects tend to belong to the third eye, throat and heart chakras. The feminine energy tends to seek a downward movement while the masculine energy tends to seek an upward movement. This is depicted by inverted triangles superposed on each other, forming a star pattern. And they meet at the heart Chakra. This Chakra is the seat of love. It is no wonder the physical union is called "Love making."

One might wonder why the female energy seeks a downward path and the male aspect seeks an upward movement. Remember that upward and downward directions have no real meaning. If one went into deep space, there is no up or down. It is just that the directions are opposite. Even the words, "male" and "female" are mere words. One can switch the two as well. We need something to denote something else. We use what is out there available to denote various things around us. The "Downward" direction refers to the tendency to experience the manifest state and the "upward" movement refers to the tendency to experience the unmanifest state.

The universe is always made up of both manifest and unmanifest existence. It is in its nature to go into manifestation and become unmanifest and vice versa. The "female" aspect is simply that which tends to manifest. The reason why it is denoted by "female" and not "male" might be due to the fact it is the female that gives birth to another individual and not the male. The manifestation of another being happens only in a female. Therefore it seems easier to denote manifestation by associating it with the female rather than the male. The two are aspects of the universe whose nature is to be dynamic, changing from one into another.

In a self realized yogi, perfect balance occurs between the masculine and feminine aspects. They exhibit both qualities at all times. Anyone who has achieved a virgin birth at the crown Chakra through the union of Kundalini with the Universal Consciousness will exhibit this inner balance. For example, when Christ was betrayed, he did not run and hide. He simply went with those who intended to punish and kill him. He knew he was going to be put to death. Yet, he did not flinch. He was beaten and made to carry the cross on his shoulders. He bled and yet did not show any fear or suffer from pain. He did not flinch and cry when he was crucified. That is an exhibition of a perfectly masculine nature. True male is not someone who exhibits his power of destruction on others in order to rule over them. A true male can control himself so much that nothing can shake him, even death. While exhibiting all the true masculine qualities, Christ also prayed for forgiveness for those who were killing him, like a dying mother would do, when shot down accidentally by her three-year-old child. He asked for compassion to those who had no awareness of what they were doing. That is perfect feminine aspect. Christ, even at the time of departure from the mortal body, exhibited a perfect balance between masculine and feminine aspects. That is the sign of a true yogi. The practice of Tantra tries to achieve this balance in various ways. Sexual union is not the only one.

Shiva is depicted as half male – half female to emphasis this truth. He also goes by the name Ardha Narishwara (the God who is half female). Balance causes neutralization of all forces involved. Equilibrium arises. Shiva is a state of complete equilibrium. Everything in nature tries to achieve balance in a field of interaction. When balance is achieved, harmony arises. Atoms align themselves in crystalline structures. Electric charges get neutralized in every atom. Planets find their orbits around their stars. Patterns emerge from balance. Geometry arises, indicating complex structures built purely through the balancing act. Everything moves until balance is achieved. Rules and laws begin to appear on their own.

Everything in the universe follows rules that are still being discovered through observations. And these rules happen because of the natural tendency to reach the state of Shiva, which is equilibrium. This is depicted as Shiva, the dancer. Tantric practice aims at achieving the same balance within.

In the Hindu system, the womb and the sexual organs are considered Divine. They are centers of creation. If one switched the view from vulgar feeling into something auspicious, imagine how it changes the view of everything in the world. Perversion and temptation would be first victims of this change. A baby suckling milk from its mother's breast is a Divine process. Not only milk, but also compassion, unconditional love and care are being transmitted into the baby from the mother. Who can see it from this new perspective? When one sees the breasts, would that bring the feelings of Divine compassion or perversion? Ask the baby first. An advanced yogi, who has overcome all human emotional limitations, would feel just like the baby. He or she would have transcended all the perverted impulses and would look at everything as innocently as a child. Women walked bare breasted in ancient India. They probably still do in tribal societies. One does not hear of violence against women in such societies. Sexual crimes are unheard of. Primitiveness is in the mind, however modern a civilization one can claim to belong to. Being "Tribal" does not make one "primitive". Innocence is Divine. The tribal is innocent and lacks sophistication and deceit that we civilized people have perfected. But his heart is a lot purer than ours. He is direct and almost childlike in his approach towards life. He lives in nature mostly and he can relate to it much better. A spiritual seeker spends a lot of time away from all civilization and dwells in caves and natural surroundings for the same reason. That is the only way to sense mother earth and see her in everything. Many yogis wear minimal clothing and some wander around completely naked in order to experience purity and oneness with nature. It alters the mindset.

Modern India and the Hinduism today have taken a somewhat conservative view of sex because of the influence from Semitic religions that ruled the sub-continent for more than a thousand years. Sex is an act of union that involves opposing poles – male and female. When it happens at the physical level, the experience is profound and is considered a Divine moment. Only ordinary humans cannot remain fully aware as they reach the ecstatic state. They have to let go of all inhibitions and allow emotions to flood their senses. There is another union that can happen at the non-physical level. It is a spiritual union. We exist in the human consciousness plane. The root Chakra in which Shakti or conscious energy resides guides our instincts. She goes by the name Kundalini. If she is allowed to traverse upward and reach the top of the crown center, known as the state of Shiva, another union takes place, giving rise to what is known as the "Virgin Birth". The same human now enters a higher consciousness plane.

Perfect balance is needed in all aspects in order to achieve this union of Shiva and Kundalini. Physical sexual union therefore is considered symbolic of the spiritual union in the Hindu religious systems. That union is known as Yog or Yoga. What is depicted in various Tantric sexual postures are in fact yogic in nature where the male and female participate in a physical union, while in different postures to exchange their mutual energies between themselves and enhance their spiritual experience. Almost every Hindu temple in Southern India has various sexual postures sculpted along the walls. No one feels vulgar about it. The feeling is the same as seeing a child naked. We love a child for lacking all inhibitions, not caring if he or she is wearing clothes or not. That nakedness radiates pure innocence. When inside a Hindu temple, despite the presence of sexual icons, devout people sense the same Divine purity. Sexual organs are worshipped and prayed to. They represent the gateway to human life.

The lingam is one such symbol. It has many definitions. In one definition, it represents an erect penis that has penetrated the vulva (yoni). Shiva is worshipped in the form of the lingam all across India. The inner sanctum in all Hindu temples is called as the "Garbha Griha", meaning the abode of birth or the womb. The womb and the lingam together represent the emergence of life from spirit.

The blockage to the mind in the form of vulgar feelings when seeing the Lingam because of what it symbolizes can leave a person trapped in worldly limitations. If on the other hand, one truly saw the Divinity in what is being symbolized, he or she can get to the next level of spiritual progress. The way one crosses over from a repulsive feeling of vulgarity to feeling the Divinity is through devotion. It is the bridge one can use to cross over human inhibitions. Those yogis and yoginis who engage in Tantric sexual acts do not seek pleasure, which is a limited experience. Their goal is to transcend the limited human emotional experience through act of physical union.

If sex is such an undesirable sin, then we all must blindfold ourselves when looking at flowers. Every flower is a sex organ in display. Everywhere along the pathway, flowers bloom and reproduction process is going on in the open, slowly of course for everyone's viewing pleasure. But we somehow seem to accept the union of male and female in flowers through the process of pollination. In nature shame does not exist. Watch little children.

They can run around naked with no inhibitions whatsoever. Pure innocence radiates from them. Their nakedness does not arouse vulgarity in the mind. They appear as pure as the flowers, don't they? And flowers radiate the same purity. That is why one does not feel vulgarity when looking at what they are intended for. In a Hindu temple, union of the male and female is given the same perspective of Divine purity. If one felt vulgar looking at them, then the task is for him to come over it and feel devotional. The image of a lingam, its bathing in white milk etc. are expected to invoke a connectivity to the creative power of the Universe in the mind of a real devotee. If one had other emotions triggered, they have a lot of work to do and come back again. All issues in the mind arise from social conditioning.

Using the physical body and environment to achieve spiritual progress and enlightenment is the meaning of Tantra. If we look around, literally everything is Tantra. It is the pathway to reach into the unmanifest using the manifest. We live and experience life in our physical bodies. If we use our body and mind to go beyond animal level existence, it is Tantra. We speak, we write, we sing, we play music, we design and do a lot of things that are beyond what our bodies need for survival and sustenance. We do use our bodies and minds to do everything beyond mere existence because something in us drives to seek such activities. It is the spirit, or Kundalini who is making us strive for seeking the unknown and challenge ourselves. The whole science of yoga and Pranayama engage in the manipulation of the body and mind to attain spiritual progress. Therefore they too belong to the school of Tantra. Sight, sound, smell, taste and tactile sensations are essential parts of our existence. Therefore the sages in India found a methodology to use these elements in spiritual pursuit. There are many ways of achieving the ultimate goal. Tantra is one of them and it can appeal to ordinary people a lot because we rely on our physical bodies and senses.

Tantra brings the extremes of physical and spiritual realms together. One is able to transcend the physical limitations and reach the unlimited realm of Universal consciousness. The droplet is able to sense the entire ocean from which it arose. The whole science of manipulating the Chakras and Nadis through various means belongs to the science of Tantra. Imagine a sealed bottle floating in the ocean containing the same seawater inside. What separates the water inside the bottle and outside is the glass enclosure. The spirit in us is the same as that Universal spirit. Connecting with the unlimited from within the limitedness of our body and mind is just like getting the water from inside the bottle to mix with what is around without breaking it. It seems magical. But has been done.

Using what we have and what is around us is the starting point of spiritual pursuit. We started at the street level where the world is perceived entirely through the limited view of the senses. Manipulation of the spiritual elements in the ethereal body happens when one steps into the temple from the street. Every temple has plenty of stimulants to trigger spiritual progress in the masses that walk through their corridors. Those stimulants work and influence the individuals in various ways based on the spiritual level of each one. We can see this clearly in the day-to-day practice of religion, rituals, festivals, functions, and activities and so on through the usage of what is around. They are called subtle elements that can be derived from objects around. Sound and geometry are such elements.

15 MANTRA AND YANTRA

We associate sound with vibrations in the air and their reception in our ears. In the context of the Hindu belief system, sound is simply that which vibrates. The hearing can be in one's ears or can be internal. Instead of the word "hearing", the word "sensing" would be more appropriate. We sense everything and hearing is just one of the senses. When vibrations are sensed internally, it is known as "Mantra" (pronounced as "Ma", "n", "thrA", with the "n" not accentuated). The word "Mun" refers to the mind, which is internal.

Syllables play an important role for Mantras. Everything has to be pronounced in a certain way with some of them having their own incantations. Sometimes Mantras take a musical form. The syllables in Mantras, when recited correctly, and sometimes at the right time and place, bring subtle vibrations from within. The power of the mantra is to trigger internal resonance with cosmic vibrations. Everything is vibration.

When I was in high school, we used to have a Physics lab experiment known as the "Resonance Bridge". A wooden bar of about two feet length is used. It has strings rigidly connected to one end. The other ends of the strings are connected to adjustable screws. The thickness and material of the strings are different. The student is asked to strike a tuning fork nearby. A tiny piece of paper is bent into a "V" shape and placed on one of the strings. The tension in the string is adjusted until at some point, the string begins to vibrate when the tuning fork is struck nearby. At the moment the paper piece would lift and fly off. This happens because the string is resonating with the vibrations of the tuning fork. When the two are matched in frequency, resonance happens. One by one the resonant frequency of each string is determined using different tuning forks. Many can tune just by listening. The material of the string, its diameter, the length, the temperature and humidity in the room etc. can affect the resonance frequency. In music terms, this is called "tuning".

When mantras are recited in a particular way, based on the spiritual status of an individual, subtle vibrations can begin to resonate within. Some mantras are initially started with oral recitation. As time goes on, they are internalized and with further practice, they run only in the mind. A steady mind is one of the conditional requirements. In addition, the practitioner has to observe certain preparation procedures. Everyone is required to bathe before sitting down to recite mantras. The direction, the time of the day, the offerings, the holding positions of fingers (known as "Mudra"), the number of times a mantra has to be recited etc. become the conditions for tuning. Mantra recitation requires regularity. The syllables making up the mantras have been created by sages during deep meditative stage and given to the disciples verbally. Every mantra is associated with a deity. The syllables are arranged to give an external meaning, while their correct pronunciation and reciting are designed to trigger internal resonance in a spiritual seeker.

Anything that triggers internal vibrations has power. Mantras are used for inner cleansing of blockages to the Nadis and Chakras. For spiritual progress, removal of the blockages is a necessary condition. Mantra chanting also relies on the devotion of the individual. Mechanical recitation has very little impact. Wandering mind also lessens the effect because correct pronunciation can be missed.

There is countless number of mantras. Every God's or deity's name itself is a mantra. Certain syllables are directly related to certain Chakras or Nadis. For example, the common Hindu name "Ram" (Pronounced as "Raam") relates to the navel Chakra whose resonant internal sound is also "Ram"). Ram is a warrior hero of the epic Ramayana who was a descendant of the solar dynasty. Sun represents fire, which is the element of the navel Chakra. His consort in the epic goes by the name "Sita" which has two meanings – one refers to furrowing and the other means "Cool".

Sita, according to the epic, is discovered in a box buried underground. The king who discovered her brings her up. Sita denotes the Kundalini who exists dormant at the root Chakra, which is related to the earthly plane or ground state. Ram represents heat (coming from the fire element) and Sita is the balancing element of cooling. I will cover more about the spiritual side of the epics. The two represent the Hot and Cold Nadis (or Solar and Lunar Nadis).

Children are given Divine names. This is so that when one calls out a child's name, they get to recite that name which is simply a mantra. The newborn child is not named immediately after birth. Typically on an auspicious day, chosen through astrological calculations, a name is chosen. Naming ceremony is a big occasion for Hindu families.

The internal influence of mantras is subtle and gradual. There are generic mantras taught to everyone. They are uttered whenever people go to temples and offer their prayers to different deities that the mantras represent. Mantras are simply vibrational representation of the Divine. Everything does not have to be in the form of an image. Generic mantras are like over-the-counter vitamin supplements. They generally benefit those who recite them with varying yields. There are certain mantras that are only taught to qualifying individuals by advanced adepts. This is because the practice and procedure have very strict guidelines of discipline and sincerity. Such mantras have tremendous power in them and can transform a seeker internally. These are kept secretive in order to prevent ego-influenced individuals from self-destructing. When one receives the power from such a mantra, if his goal is not spiritual progress, he can abuse what he has attained and invite terrible karma and suffering to those around him. We saw this in the story of the lion at the beginning. There are many such stories in India where people started out with sincerity and ego crept in somewhere along their path and they fell.

The traditional way of teaching mantras is strictly verbal. One is discouraged from writing them down. This is because written script cannot exactly express all the subtle modulations in voice and pronunciation. One of the most ancient scriptures of India, the Vedas were passed down from generation to generation through oral recitation under the guidance of masters. Those who practiced these mantras were expected to be righteous, honest, ethical, moral and spiritual in their belief and conduct. The blessings of the master were extremely important. One learned through experience rather than reference.

Many powerful mantras have been deliberately kept away from public usage because of their effects and reach. One has to earn the privilege to learn them from an experienced master. There are generic versions of some of these mantras available. The syllables have been structured in such a way to minimize any harm. One of them is the "Gayathri Mantra" (pronounced as "Gaa yath ri").

The generic version of the Gayathri mantra is recited everywhere in India. It forms a part of the Rig Veda. It is a mantra taught to young males (typically at the age of six) as a part of a ceremony. A master teaches the mantra. In ancient India, once the mantra was taught, the boy left the family to live with the guru and learn. He returned after learning all the scriptures and was ready for marriage at the age of eighteen. The guru was given an offering as a token of appreciation. In ancient India, teaching was done traditionally this way. Students learned different skills. Those who belonged to the warrior class learned the skills of archery, wrestling, sword fighting, making war strategies, codes of conduct etc. Those who came from the priestly class were taught rituals, prayers, procedures etc. Men who recite the Gayathri mantra are required to wear a cotton thread that loops from the left shoulder to the right side of the hip. It has specific number of knots and has to be made up of a certain type of cotton. The Gayathri Mantra has the power to generate internal heat if the conditions become proper. A male reciting the mantra under those conditions can experience tremendous heat build up. Many times people would stand in hip deep water in order to recite it. Though it appears simply ritualistic, there is always a chance for the one amongst the millions to experience this internal heat[2].

The other generic mantra is the Ganesh mantra. This mantra is recited at the start of anything in order to provide guidance and removal of any obstacles that can appear. The syllables are arranged in a way to trigger vibrations at the root chakra that help stabilize the mind, which is needed for executing any task. Ganesh is considered the gatekeeper of the root chakra. Reciting this mantra also sets up subtle vibrations that can help open up the Sushumna Nadi to allow the passage of Kundalini upward. Earlier in this book I had narrated the story of how Ganesh got an elephant head. It was a narration at the street level. At the inner level, it has a different narration. The Sushumna Nadi is always sealed in ordinary people. Kundalini remains dormant at the root chakra. In the story of Ganesh, she is known as Parvati, his mother. Ganesh was asked to stay on guard while she bathed. Ganesh followed the order so sincerely that he would not even allow his father, Shiva to enter. And so goes the story. Ganesh mantra helps in removing the seal of the Sushumna Nadi.

It must be said that for ordinary people, it is better for this Nadi to remain sealed. For Kundalini to move upward through this Nadi, one must be prepared. She is like a river held up by a huge dam. If the dam bursts for any reason, the flood cannot be controlled. The accidental release of Kundalini can sometimes be a frightening experience for the unprepared. All blockages to Nadis and Chakras must be cleared prior to her ascent. Otherwise the liberated Kundalini will try to clear the blockages or find alternative paths through the network of 72000 Nadis, while not reaching the crown seat of Shiva. This can cause mental sickness or pain and suffering that no medicine can easily diagnose or cure. Ganesh mantra also protects a devotee from accidentally opening the Sushumna Nadi. When one is ready, the obstacle will be dissolved and the ascent of Kundalini will happen.

People today dispute the existence of God. There is an easy way to address this. If God represents not a person but an experience, the whole meaning changes. Many deities depicted in Hindu systems are descriptions of an internal experience. Goddess Kali is one such representation. She takes a frightening form. She drinks blood. She wears a garland of human skulls. She carries a sword. Our image of God is that of a loving, and merciful old man with a beard. But here God is depicted in a form that is undesirable to many. The reason is simple. It depicts an inner experience. Amongst all fears, the most frightening fear in every human being is that of dying. If we suddenly face death, it can be a profound experience. When a seeker is not ready yet to receive the cosmic experience and it happens through wrongful practice or unexpectedly, Kundalini will try to find a path to the seat of Shiva. If blockages are present on her path, the experience arising out of that hindrance to her movement can cause a frightening experience. That experience is depicted in the form of Kali or Durga. It is the same Divinity. But when experienced through a different path, it takes the frightening form[3] . If one manages to clear the blockage, the same Kali now transforms into Saraswati, the seat of wisdom and love.

Kali   **Saraswati**

When blockages are present, the Kundalini tries to unblock them. There have been observations of people swinging their bodies widely or perspiring profusely and having a panting breath. People have mentioned about feeling a deafening water fall like sound or feeling thousands of ants crawling all over their bodies. Some people automatically assume postures that resemble yogic postures. In fact the science of yoga was developed by observing such phenomena. Some breathe in ways that differ from normal breathing. These experiences are difficult to explain or depict. Once the blockage gets removed through the guidance of an adept, a seeker experiences bliss. Such people can sense the astral aura around all manifested objects and beings.

There are innumerable mantras that are recited in all Hindu temples by priests at different times of the day. Mantras are also specific to different rituals like marriages, anniversaries, festivals, celebrations, funerals and so on. Fire is an important aspect of every ritual around which mantras are recited. Fire pits are constructed according to specific geometric patterns. Fire is an element of transformation. Cow dung and wood from specific trees native to the land are used for burning. Clarified butter is poured to increase the flames. A special type of grass (Eragrostis cynosuroides) is used in all these rituals. Mantras are chanted loud. This process is known as Yaga or Yagnya where the chants are addressed to the deity of interest. Yagnyas are held to ward off negativity and to maintain the spiritual purity of the place and the people. Mantras play a very important role.

There are mantras for different purposes. Some are made up of single syllables. These are also known as "Bhija" mantras. These are mantras that appeared during deep meditation and were given by the guru to the disciple. Each Chakra has its own Bhija mantra. Reciting them or hearing them can help the chakras to resonate and tune. The mantra "Aum" is known as the primordial mantra. It is the vibration sensed when a yogi attains the state of self-realization as the Kundalini leaves the root chakra and traverses the Sushumna Nadi and reaches the seat of the Universe above the crown of the head. The mantra resulting from the union of Shiva and Shakti at the crown Chakra is "Aum". The Sanskrit script for this mantra resembles the number 3.

The dot and a crescent moon like symbol at the top right denotes the "m" sound that never ends. It is also known as the "Bindu". According to Tantra, Bindu Visarga (which means "the falling of the drop") is a point at the mid-brain. It represents consciousness. Brahmin priests wear the tufts. The tuft is tightly tied at the spot above the Bindu Visarga. The flow of the fluid from this spot can be manipulated by a yogi to prolong his physical life for enhancing spiritual practice. This symbol is shown with the image of Shiva.

The Aum symbol also resembles the head of an elephant seen sideways. This explains the elephant head of Lord Ganesh who is represented by the symbol "Aum". He is the son of Shiva and Parvati. When Kundalini reaches the crown chakra and unites with Shiva, the Universal consciousness, the vibration that emerges is Ganesh, symbolized by the elephant head. Ganesh is the keeper of the root chakra, which refers to the earthly plane of consciousness. Ganesh symbolically represents the link between the human and universal consciousness. The Hindu system is based on the principle that every being is internally connected to the Cosmos. All the spiritual practices are means to realize that connectivity. Every droplet that splits from the ocean still carries the same properties as the ocean water.

One really cannot provide the physical proof of a God's existence. Nor can one describe its characteristics. That which can only be realized through inner experience is extremely difficult to describe or explain. However, symbolic representation has been used to simply provide a means to experience within oneself and understand it. Tantra has many methods to reach this inner realm. Mantras enhance the process. Yantras are yet another set of tools that are used for the same purpose, albeit in a limited way. Yantra is simply a deity expressed in a geometric pattern instead of an image of a person. Everything in the spiritual realm can be approached using Tantra or Mantra or Yantra or all of them combined. Yantra also means a machine or a tool. The patterns include various combinations of straight lines, petals, circles, triangles and squares. Each one represents the energetic vibration.

The circle and straight line represent the energy vibrations of the water element. The square represents the earthly vibrations. An upward facing triangle represents the fire element (Agni). A downward facing triangle represents water element. A diagonal line represents the air element (Vayu). A point denotes the ethereal element (Akash). Yantras are another method of representing the Deities. For example, Ganesh is represented by the Hindu Swastika symbol.

Sri Yantra   **Kali Yantra**

Instead of a deity in the human or animal form, Yantras represent the deity in the geometric form. Deities are gateways into higher levels of consciousness. Each Yantra carries a specific vibrational energy. By focusing on the Yantra one can find access to higher planes of consciousness. These geometric patterns, like mantras, were received during deep meditation. They were not imagined. Each pattern induces a specific resonant vibration in the spiritual practitioner. Mantra acts as a link between the individual spirit and the Universal one. Mental focus is achieved by meditating on the Yantra. One focuses at the center of the Yantra and with increased practice begins the process of spiritual elevation. In Buddhism, Yantras are referred to as Mandalas. It is a traditional practice in Southern India to draw Yantra patterns on the ground in front of homes, inside houses and at temples.

Yantras are energized by proper rituals and chanting of mantras. Not only Yantras, everything in the religious system gets energized. After the construction of a temple, the deity inside is energized through rituals. Energizing is the process by which the cosmic energy is drawn into the deity that can be in the form of a stone idol or a yantra.

I have presented many things so far in a sequence that I have used to understand the system in which I grew up. I have come across many things during my formative years and I never understood the underlying reasons and connectivity between them. Those who did not know much, but were in an honorable position as wise elders tried to talk about them in an exotic manner in order not to make much sense, both to themselves and to the others. Many made up their own theories that they defended through arguments with others. Going inward is something most had no idea about or thought of trying. There are thousands of things that I can go on listing in this book about more exotic things. However, that is not the purpose. One can find the meaning behind many of these rituals, elements and beliefs just by looking inward. I will explain it through the concept of the circle.

16 THE CIRCLE AND THE STRAIGHT LINE

We Indians are credited for giving to the world nothing. And I am very proud of it. The number zero in today's mathematics denotes nothing. Without symbols we cannot approach anything. Every number is a symbol that represents a quantity. In religions a symbol can represent an entity.

Every letter in a language is a symbol denoting a sound. We exist by relying on symbols. So "Nothing" is also denoted by a symbol that resembles a circle. One might wonder why a square or a triangle or a straight-line was not chosen to represent this value of nothing. Most symbols came into existence through philosophical contemplation. There is a reason why a symbol represents a certain thing. The symbol "Aum" is represented in a certain way to denote not only a sound, but also an internal experience. No one knows when the concept of zero came about or who "invented" it. There is no historical record of when exactly this symbol was first introduced. But it is known that the concept of nothing and its symbolic representation by a circle arose in India. From a mathematical standpoint, it made things much easier. Huge numbers could now be written using a series of zeros. This symbol was adopted by the Arabs who later introduced it in Medieval Europe.

Let us look at the realization of "nothing". To us humans, the idea of nothing gives some level of discomfiture. It feels as though we are blind folded and left to wander with no sense of orientation. "Nothing" is an absolute term. Anything that is not manifest can be termed as nothing. But there is matter that is invisible to our eyes and other senses. The air is invisible because it is colorless. We can sense it because we can feel the wind and are breathing it all the time. Energy does not have a shape or any definite appearance. But we can sense energy and its transmission through matter. Nothing is even beyond energy. It simply has no manifestation in any form. Does such a thing really exist? If something of that kind has to exist, how can it be called "nothing"? That is against the very idea of it. So what is nothing? Is it a relative term? We can say that empty space can be termed as nothing. How do we know it is empty?

Anything that we cannot sense can appear empty. If one looked up in the night sky, we do see plenty of empty space studded with stars and matter. Using sophisticated telescopes, it has been observed that all these matter that we see in the sky are of enormous dimension and these massive objects are separated by distances that are even more enormous. There is plenty of space where no matter might be visible. Every form of matter seems to be floating in empty space that is much larger in dimension. Everything seems to exist in nothing. And this nothing seems to be infinite in dimension. How can something that is nothing, which can be infinite? This is the philosophical question. If one attempted to answer this question, he could spend his entire life on it and still would get nothing as an answer.

The ancient sages decided simply to accept whatever that is and gave it a symbol. It is a circle. Now one might wonder how a circle became a symbol for that. Let us look at this philosophical approach towards just describing not just nothing, but also its relationship to everything and the infinite. How can one represent something that is nothing and is infinite? Here is how it works.

Let us imagine a large circle in an empty space. The size of the diameter can be anything. Within the circle there is nothing. The perimeter of the circle is finite. One can measure it. A circle can be imagined as a polygon of infinitesimally small sides. That is how the circumference of a circle is calculated. A circle is a polygon with infinite number of sides. The sides are so infinitesimally small that they appear like dots. Infinite number of sides form a circumference of finite length that surrounds nothing. Outside of the perimeter there is nothing as well. Thus a finite shape denoted by a circle has nothing both inside and outside of it. Nothing surrounds a finite length that has infinite number of segments in it. We know that every circle has a center, which comes into being because of the line that makes its perimeter. Every point on the perimeter is equidistant from this center. This equality represents perfect balance.

If forces existed that pulled each other in opposing directions and with equal magnitude, they would create a balance. Anything that achieves this balance in all directions will only form one shape – the circular one. Every star and planet in cosmos is spherical in shape because of a balance between the internal forces that push outward and gravity. Objects settle into a circular orbit around their common center of gravity as well. Amongst all geometric objects, only the circle has this unique characteristic of representing nothing, infinity, finiteness and balance. Other geometric objects might have symmetry, but they will not fit all these philosophical definitions. Thus a circle came to represent nothing that is infinite in nature. In Sanskrit it was called Shunya (pronounced as "Shoo", "nya") and the numeral was called Pujya (pronounced as "Poo", "jya").

Nothingness also represents a state of experience. When self-realization happens, one enters a state of complete inner balance. Buddhists call it nakedness or "Nirvana". One can fully experience and understand the true meaning of what nothingness means in that state. In Sanskrit it is also called as "Shunyata". Everything arises from nothing at a fundamental level. Everything also exists in nothing.

The circle also has another interesting philosophical meaning to it. If one stands on the perimeter of a circle and decided to reach the farthest point from where he stands, he would walk forward, complete the full circle and reach his farthest point, which was the one from where he started. It is the beginning and it is the end. If, instead of going forward, he simply looked inward and stayed where he was, he would have accomplished the same thing. Going forward represents our outward looking experience and learning from it. Staying at the same place and looking inward simply brings the realization of everything. The forward movement represents sense based outward approach. The inward approach is meditation. The circle represents the unmanifest aspect of the Universe.

Like the circle, the next most significant symbol is One. In different societies "one" might be represented by various symbols. The one we are familiar with is the vertical line. It simply represents the quantity of something and not its magnitude. Every number, other than zero, is an addition of one, all the way to infinity. All multiplication is based on addition. At the fundamental level, there are only two numbers out of which every other number has been constructed – one and zero. One represents something that exists and zero represents nothing. The two thus represent the manifest and unmanifest nature of the Universe.

The manifest part of the Universe brings boundaries and limits to everything. It also brings duality into the picture. Relative dimensions come into existence. References and orientation become necessary. Rules come into play. Forces arise. Balance becomes necessary. Simple builds up the complex. The first duality in this Universe is its manifest and unmanifest aspects. Both exist side by side. In the vastness of cosmos, atoms, rocks, planets, stars and galaxies exist, separated by empty space. Inside tiny atoms, the same nothingness is present where the sub-atomic particles are separated by empty space. Nothingness seems to penetrate into everything that is manifest. Everything that is manifest seems to fill into the empty space. They both are intertwined. In the dualistic vision, that which is manifest can only be sensed or realized in relational reference to the unmanifest. One can only be defined with respect to zero. However, nothingness needs no reference. If one experiences nothingness or nirvana, he understands a non-referential state of absolute existence that cannot be sensed from the dualistic viewpoint.

Everything is built on one and zero. If one multiplied one an infinite number of times, it is still one. No other number has this unique characteristic. And zero would neutralize any number into zero if multiplied by it. This includes one as well. The unmanifest contains everything. One, being denoted by a straight vertical line, shows extremes as separated apart from each other. The symbol's base starts at one extreme and ends at the other. This represents the view of the mortal mind where extremes always exist. There is good and evil. There is day and night. There is hot and cold. There is pain and pleasure. There is happiness and sorrow. There is love and hatred. There is light and darkness. There is past and the future. We can distinctly see the two apart. We live in the world of extremes. We always like one over the other. This is the characteristic of the manifest world. That is why the perception is always to seek One God, one origin of everything and the tendency to have one religion for all. The manifest always seeks an answer in the manifest. It is a natural tendency.

In the Hindu philosophical standpoint, zero is Shiva and one is Shakti. The two aspects together define the Universe. One represents a state and the other, the conscious experience of that state. Shiva symbolizes the most fundamental state of nothingness where everything emanates from. It also represents a state of neutrality or complete balance. Without Shakti, experience cannot happen. She is both the observer and the experience of the observation. I am using the terms, "He" and "She" here for easy reading. Shakti constantly arises from Shiva, experiences everything and continuously reunites with Shiva. Awareness builds in this process. This is something that has no beginning or an end, much like one can never point to a starting point on the perimeter of a circle. It is a continuous process. It has no beginning or end, but cyclical. At each end, a new beginning arises and it moves on and on. It is thus termed as an eternal dance or cosmic dance.

When complete awareness arises through manifest experience, that state is simply called as the state of Brahma, the state of complete wisdom or Saraswati. There is no difference between Brahma and Shiva or Shakti and Saraswati. It just makes it easier for us to understand the process because we can only look at the infinite from a finite standpoint. We need to denote everything by a name or a symbol, just to make it easier for us to get a better perspective of everything.

Names have no meaning in the realm of "Nothing". We could call it Nothing and Something instead of Shiva and Shakti. They are just names. Of course people would find it difficult to relate to anything that is abstract. They like to see everything in human terms. It is made easier by Vishnu and Lakshmi.

Amongst the three Gods of the Holy Trinity of modern Hinduism, Vishnu plays the role that people relate to the most. He incarnates in many forms, including human forms. He romances, suffers, betrays, fights, conquers, guides and liberates through various incarnations. Vishnu also represents a state of existence, the world of duality. Lakshmi represents everything that is manifest. Shiva, Vishnu and Brahma represent Universal Consciousness that appears split across a spectrum of consciousness planes. Shiva forms the most fundamental state of consciousness on one end. Brahma represents the other end. Everything else in between is Vishnu. Everything is as it is. All planes of consciousness exist at all times. The Universal God can be simply called as Consciousness, which is made of two components – Experience and Consciousness. Shakti represents the experience and Shiva represents the consciousness. Together they enable awareness. Or we can substitute Lakshmi and Vishnu or Saraswati and Brahma and the meaning will not change.

It is in our nature to view the universe from a dualistic perspective. We cannot survive without relational reference frames. We will go insane. From that reference frame, it is all right to describe the absolute on referential terms. When we do, Gods and their consorts come into existence. The tiny droplets get a sense of the vast ocean they come from. In our relational frame of mind, we need a point of origin at all times. Relative to that origin everything can be understood. That origin can be nothing. In this Cartesian reference frame, we can orient ourselves and try to understand the Universe in as simplistic steps as possible. The simplest step can be a unit that we call as "one". This brings us to the world of numbers. Numbers are an essential part of our referential existence. Each number is related to the other. We need measurements and quantification. Without numbers we cannot achieve them. Anything we define assumes a shape, a certain dimension and characteristics. Numbers are an integral part in that process. The science of Astrology simply cannot exist without numbers. And Astrology forms an integral part of Hindu religious systems.

17 THE WORLD OF NUMBERS

Numbers play an important part in many religious systems in the world. The Hindu systems are no exception. Hindu religions and Astrology are so tightly interconnected that numbers and calculations have become an integral part of everything. Numbers are not looked at as merely abstract entities. Every number has a significant philosophical meaning and some numbers have a spiritual significance. The syllables used to denote those numbers add to the inner vibrations. In many ritual chants the numbers will be recited. In many vernacular educational systems in India, mathematical operations are taught at the elementary school level through a chanting process. Addition, multiplication, fraction etc. are taught by repetitive chanting. The intuitive element is sharpened when basics are taught in the form of chanting. The entire Indian classical music system is taught orally and through repetition. One is discouraged from writing things down. This is not the process today because of Westernization of the Indian educational system and the advancement in technology. However, the effective use of numbers, their underlying meaning etc. were once taught through oral traditions.

In a famous ritual chant known as "Chamakam", numbers are recited first with odd numbers from one to 33 and then even numbers in multiples of 4 up to 48. Each number refers to specific spiritual elements some of which are discussed as follows.

The number two represents the objective and subjective experience in the manifest world. There is the observer and there is the object that is being observed. With our senses directed outward, it is natural for one to see the two as distinctly apart. The word "dual" refers to two – the observer and the observed, and everything and its exact opposite. While "One" also symbolizes two opposites that cannot meet, it mainly represents the manifest more than anything else. Two really gives the dimension for duality in the manifest world. Separation is an aspect of the dualistic world.

Each fish appears separate from the others and distinct from the water in which it is swimming. However, no fish can survive out of water. If one cannot survive outside of something, then that something, be it internal or external, becomes a part of it. We cannot live without blood in our bodies. Blood flows internally. Thus it is a part of each one of us. However, the air we breathe comes from outside of us. We cannot survive without air either. Though it is external to us, our complete reliance on it makes it a part of our lives. It may not be part of our bodies all the time, but it sure is a part of our lives. The question is then, which is the important one - The body or the life? What is a body worth without life? And what becomes of life without a body? The two are inseparable. When they separate, we call it death. Until death doeth them apart, we are dependent on internal and external means to survive.

Thus what is outside of each individual becomes a part of that individual as long as they rely on it. But the perception is as though we are separate from everything observing everything around us. It is because of the wiring in us. We cannot help perceive the world around us that way. If we stretch this analysis further, we need to earth to survive. We need a base to live on that holds us together. Thus earth becomes a part of us. We cannot survive without the light and heat from the sun. When we imbibe sun's energy to survive, it becomes a part of us and we become a part of its system.

Though we see the sun as a separate entity that is 93 million miles away from us, we cannot exist without the sun. When we cannot exist without something, it becomes us. We cannot exist without our bodies, can we? If our bodies are us, then so is the air, water, earth, sun and the whole Universe. Two represents the objective and subjective experience.

In the Hindu system, the temporary separation of the droplet from the ocean is accepted. The droplet has the same salinity, density and other physical characteristics of the grand ocean from which it becomes separate temporarily. This example is used to explain the individual soul (Atman) and the Universal soul (Brahman). Two represents these two states where the atman appears separate from the Brahman temporarily and then merges with it. Atman has all the qualities of the Brahman. When it exists in a physical plane where referential frames and duality exist, it appears as though it is distinctly different from everything of which it becomes a part.

Two represents dualism. In the real world that we are familiar with, our existence is based on our sense perceptions. We orient ourselves with respect to a reference frame. In a referential system, everything is perceived in relation to something else. Day cannot be realized without the night. Light cannot be realized without darkness. Summer cannot be realized without winter. Hot cannot be understood without cold. Though the two extremes appear opposite, they compliment each other. We need both to orient ourselves. If we enter a realm where references become irrelevant then one experiences the absence of dualism. It happens in the internal experience that does not rely on the senses. Sense withdrawal is one of the steps in yogic traditions to enter that realm.

Three is an important number. There are three worlds (Tri-loka) – earthly, higher and lower planes of existence. There are three eyes (Tri-ambaka) – two physical and one spiritual. This is symbolically represented in Hindu rituals using the coconut. It has three spots that represent the three eyes. In many rituals, the coconut will be placed upside down over a brass pot filled with water (coconut represents the human head and the pot filled with water, the body of a human).

The triangle with three sides is a symbol that is extensively used in Hindu systems. The upward pointing triangle is the drive for the unmanifest. The downward pointing triangle is the drive to manifest. Triangle forms an important element for Mantra meditation. The Supreme Gods in the Hindu system represent the three aspects of everything in the Universe – Emergence (Brahma), Sustaining (Vishnu) and Dissolution (Shiva), the three states of consciousness.

Three represents the basic qualities in humans – Sattva (enlightened), Tamas (ignorant) and Rajas (intermediate). The Trident is associated with many deities in Hinduism. The three prongs of the trident represent the three qualities in humans. The Divine is beyond the three. By holding the trident on its hands, the Deity is symbolically describing the state of beyond these three human states.

Time scale is divided into three as well – Past, Present and the Future. In the world of reference, the three appear distinctly separate. People can be categorized into three groups based on their biological constitution (Dosha). They are known as Vata, Pitta and Kapha. A person with a Vata constitution is usually thin, quick and agile. Pitta constitution reflects a fiery and energetic temperament. Kapha people are quiet, solid and firm.

Four represents the four primary directions in this referential world of ours. In the Hindu belief system, four has more meanings. There are four Vedas (Rg, Yajur, Sama and Atharva). There are four classes of people (Varna) based on their inherent nature – Shudra, Vaisya, Khshatriya and Brahman. Unfortunately, corruption of the system became inevitable and these four classes were rigidly imposed to hold on to power and influence over the others. These four classifications are natural tendencies in each human. All four exist in every individual to varying degrees and they vary according to circumstances. Each person is dominated by one of these tendencies based on his birth (inherent) and conditions. One, who prefers to be ignorant and lives for materialistic rewards, has no awareness or desire for anything beyond mere existence is known to be dominated by the Shudra tendency. One who is enlightened is dominated by the Brahman tendency. The other two intermediate stages show the gradation from Shudra to Brahman tendencies. People with similar tendencies tend to attract and group.

There are four eras (Yuga), which go in a cyclical fashion – Satya, Treta, Dwapara and Kali. And these correspond to the four tendencies described in the above paragraph. Kali Yuga is an age of darkness (Tamas) where Shudra tendencies dominate. Satya Yuga is the age of enlightenment. The beings that exist during each era arise due to their own natural tendencies. The time scale for each one varies based on what the source of reference is. We know that we undergo four seasons during a year. There are festivals corresponding to each season because agriculture depends on the seasons.

Five (Pancha) represents many things. There are five senses (vision, hearing, smell, taste and tactile). There are five elements (earth, water, fire, air and spirit) associated with a body that experiences living. The Hindu calendar is called "Panchanga" because it relies on five elements – thithi (position of the sun), vara (day of the week), nakshatra (star position), karan (moon's position) and saguna (auspicious moment). The life force has five functions – Prana (incoming), Apana (outgoing), Samana (digestive), Udana (upward moving) and Vyana (sense, coordination and balance).

Seven is a very significant number. Classical music in India has seven notes corresponding to the Western classical music. Each note corresponds to a frequency of sound, with higher notes corresponding to higher frequency. In a system that considers everything to be in the form of vibrations, there are seven primary chakras along the human spine, each with an increased vibrational frequency compared to the previous one. The human body can be compared to a musical instrument. Just having seven notes does not make the piano worthy of anything. It is when the notes are played deftly by an accomplished musician do they come alive. One does not realize subtle variations, tempos and melodies until the pianist plays the keys. The piano now becomes a device to express the inner experience of the musician who breathes life into it. The Chakras in our bodies are active to varying degrees, being played by the life force and energy.

There are seven days in a week, with each day corresponding to a celestial body. Two such weeks correspond to the waxing and waning cycles of the moon, making up a lunar month. There is a famous temple for Vishnu in Southern India that is denoted by its location on what is known as the "Seven Hills" (Sapta Giri). Hindu astrology refers to the seven sages (Sapta Rishi) who are referred to by the seven stars in the Ursa Major constellation. According to the astronomical time scale in the Hindu system, during each time period known as the Manvantara, seven sages appear. Seven is also the number of visible colors of the optical spectrum ranging from red to violet. The God in the Rg Veda, Indra holds a bow that is made up of the rainbow that has the seven colors. The bow is symbolically used in Hindu mythology to represent the human spine. The colors indicated correspond to the colors of the Chakras along the spine. One will find in many Hindu myths, heroes being great archers. The bow represents the spine and the archer refers to the spiritual seeker.

There are seven primary Chakras that define the human who can vary in nature from an animalistic state to highly enlightened state. Corresponding to each Chakra, there is a plane of consciousness (Loka) – Earthly, mid earthly, heavenly, radiant world, world of deities, world of advanced souls and the world of truth.

In addition to the four primary directions, there are four secondary directions (North East, South West, North West and South East), making eight directions. According to Patanjali, there are eight stages to self realization (Discipline, Rules, Postures, Breathing exercise, Sense withdrawal, Concentration, Meditation and Self Realization).

The Hindu Astrological system refers to nine celestial bodies (seven are observable to the human eye, the last two are ethereal – Rahu and Ketu). The human body has 9 entrances – Mouth, Two Nostrils, Two Ears, Two Eyes, and Two elimination openings). According to the traditional temple building codes (Agama Shastra), the laying of the foundation involves placing nine jewels and nine types of grains. Nine represents renewal. The Sanskrit word for nine is "Nava" which also means new (Indo-European word).

Twelve is another important number in the Hindu religious systems. The Hindu Astrological system refers to 12 zodiacs (same constellations as in the Egyptian/Greek system), through which the sun goes through each day. There are twelve months in the Hindu Lunar calendar as well.

The moon takes 14 days of waxing and waning, completing a full lunar month. According to the spiritual traditions, there are fourteen planes of consciousness (7 below the earthly plane. The other seven were mentioned earlier). These also correspond to the 7 Chakras along the human spine and 7 more along the legs and hands.

One hundred and Eight is an extremely auspicious numbers as well. There are 108 holy places of Lord Vishnu across the land. Many mantra chants are said 108 times. From the Hindu Astrology standpoint, there are 9 celestial bodies that go through 12 zodiacs (houses), the product of which is 108. The heart Chakra is said to have the convergence of 108 Nadis. An interesting side note for 108 is the ratio of the Distance between the sun and the earth to the Sun's diameter. The distance is 93 million miles. And Sun's diameter is 865000 miles. This might be a mere coincidence. If one divided the earth-moon distance by the moon's diameter, it also comes close to 108. It is not known if the ancient Indians knew about the heliocentric solar system or whether earth was a sphere etc.

The ratio of the different bodies and their distances being almost the same is an interesting observation. We will call it a mere coincidence, just like how the moon exactly covers the entire sun during a solar eclipse. Its distance is such that when it crosses the line of sight between the earth and the sun, it ends up covering the sun completely! If one used the concept of similar triangles, then this interesting coincidence will no longer be one. It is highly mathematical. If there are two isosceles triangles with a common apex (earth) that have the same ratio of height to base lengths, then the base of one (moon's disc) will completely cover the base of the other (sun's disc) when viewed from the apex.

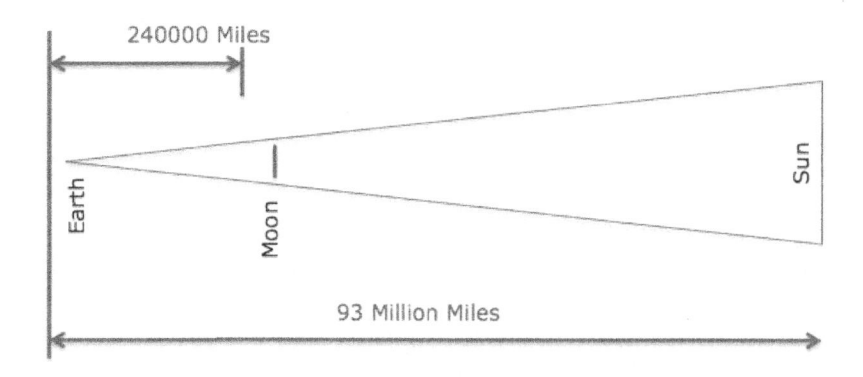

According to the yogic system in India, there are 108 locations in the astral body where the Nadis cross each other. These are called as Chakras. They are spread all over the astral body, corresponding to one's spine, hands, legs and other parts. Chanting mantras with 108 beads is meant to help tune these Chakras. People go around certain deities 108 times.

The eclipse is considered an auspicious event across India. On these occasions, calculated using astrological charts, some people observe fast and bathe in rivers. Men belonging to the Brahmin caste chant the Gayathri mantra. It is the occasion when the sun and the moon come together. While there are the physical sun and the moon, there are also corresponding ethereal Nadis that go by the same name in the human. The two Nadis (Ida and Pingala or Solar and Lunar) converge at a location near the base of the spine and also come together near the nostrils. Performing the Pranayama exercise, observing fast, standing in a flowing river or stream and chanting the Gayathri mantra are meant to generate spiritual vibrations inside an aspirant which can help open the Sushumna Nadi. This may not happen in everyone who follows these rituals religiously. However, there might always be one who could be ripe for that transformation. The sun corresponds to the masculine aspects and the moon corresponds to the feminine aspects. When the two come together, by following the ritualistic procedures one can achieve inner balance between these two aspects. I had earlier discussed about the male-female balance in yogis. The Eclipse is this both external and internal. The Hindu religious beliefs are centered on the cosmic connectivity between mortals and the Universe.

It is important to mention the religious-spiritual background of numbers. The Hindu system has the core belief that everything is spiritual, even numbers. It is difficult to tell the religion apart from astrology. The two are so well intertwined that astrology forms an important foundation of Hindu religious systems. Religion and belief based practices are the means to enhance one's spiritual progress. However, progress happens based on one's awareness, ability to choose wisely and deeds. People follow traditional practices during important rituals that use these numbers. For example, when marriage rituals involve the fire, the bride and the groom go around it 9 times. Circling around a holy place, be it a fire pit or a temple, is done nine times.

Astrological events and cycles define the various eras. The Gods are not considered eternal. All Gods appear during each era known as the Life of Brahma, which is made into 36000 divisions known as the Kalpa, or a day for Brahma. Each Kalpa is further divided into 14 days and 15 nights. The days, known as "Manvantaras" (Manu's time period) are further divided into 4 time periods known as Yuga (Satya, Treta, Dwapara and Kali). The number of earth years quoted for each one varies. According to the

charts, we are currently living during the end of Kali Yuga, belonging to the 7th day (Manvantara). A Brahma cycle thus is a gigantic number.

Everything listed so far is not meant to justify anything or boasting. Every culture has something to offer and has done amazing things in the world. It is just that the Hindu system looks complicated to the untrained eye. If one understood the basic structure of it and used that structure to navigate his way through the system, its understanding becomes a lot clearer. It is like music. The entire music system has its fundamental structure on only 7 notes. There is an infinite variation possible using these 7 notes. Likewise, I am showing the fundamental aspects of the Hindu religious system, out of which many combinations and variations have evolved. It is easier to understand the basic structure from which everything has been derived rather than try to observe it from what has evolved to where it is. We are trying to look at the tree at its very root rather than through each branch of it.

18 ELEMENTS

One of the most fundamental tenets in all Hindu systems is that there is a Divine element in everything around. Those elements can be used to connect with our own inner Divinity and enhance spiritual progress, knowingly or unknowingly.

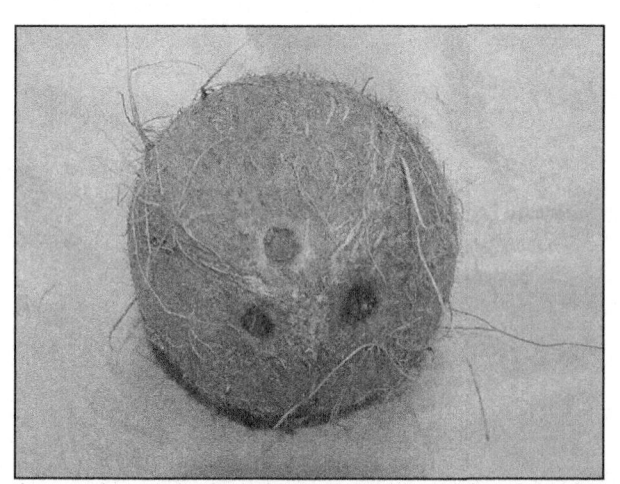

India is a sub-tropical nation. Coconut is in abundance. It is an extremely important element in the Hindu belief systems. It symbolically represents the human skull. There is a hard shell that contains the white flesh inside. It has three dark spots at the bottom, representing the three eyes on a human face (two that are normal eyes and the third one being an eye for wisdom). A coconut is compared to Shiva's head in an old Tamil poem. Shattering the coconut symbolizes the breaking up of ignorance and revelation of a higher consciousness within. This symbolic act is performed in front of many Ganesh temples. However, those who shatter coconuts are not doing so to liberate themselves from ignorance. They are practical and want a piece of it and it is fun.

Coconuts are used in every Hindu ritual. A coconut is placed with its fibrous tail facing upwards on top of a pot filled with water. The two together represent the head and the body. Every ceremony that deals with marriage, childbirth, house warming, birthdays etc. involves the coconut placed on top of the water filled pot. Nowadays most people leave these things to the priests and simply go through the rituals. The priests bring in all the needed materials or have them arranged to be brought and people simply attend the rituals, waiting for it to end so that they could go to eat.

Vermilion plays an extremely important role in the Hindu systems as well. It is a sign of auspiciousness. Its red color relates to the root Chakra. It is typically worn on the forehead, where the third eye is situated. The human body, according to the Hindu astrological system, has locations corresponding to the twelve zodiacs. The location of the third eye where the vermilion is applied corresponds to the Aries zodiac. The Lord of this house is Mars, which is a red planet. At the street level, most people just wear the vermillion on their foreheads and today it has become exclusively for women, excepting for widows. Every deity in the Hindu belief system wears the vermilion on the forehead. It is the sign of auspiciousness.

Turmeric is another auspicious element used in every ritual. Turmeric paste is applied around the vermillion on the forehead, as well as other parts of the body. Turmeric comes in both amber and yellow colors, amber color corresponding to the Chakra in the sacral region and yellow corresponding the Chakra in the navel region. It has the regenerative and transformational elements. It is one of the main spices used in Indian cooking. Turmeric has several medicinal applications as well.

Every deity is worshipped with lighted camphor. The smell of burning camphor is significant. It corresponds to the smell sensation experienced internally when the third eye chakra becomes active or energized when someone does yoga or Pranayama exercises. As a corollary, if there is someone amongst the masses offering prayer at a temple, it is possible through mere coincidence to have his or her third eye chakra activated as camphor smell is sensed during the prayer ritual. Every element used in temples and rituals corresponds to chakras and Nadis. Every deity does the same.

Fire or Agni represents transformation. It is a process by which matter transforms into energy and vice versa. In our own bodies, what we consume is transformed at the cellular level into life sustaining energy. So long as the process of Agni runs in us, our body temperature remains steady and we remain alive in our bodies. Agni is also an element for spiritual transformation. When a person is transformed through the process of Agni, he becomes a spiritual seeker. His navel chakra is activated. However, this is the stage to seek guidance. Unguided attempts can become unsuccessful because temptations and habits from the lower chakras will rise up with a vengeance. Those who have the navel chakra becoming active are like warriors about to launch into the war or conflict. They have to be extremely alert and have a pursuit as single minded and sharp like the tip of an arrow at the hands of a warrior. This is the David stage where the mighty Goliath stands, bringing all buried temptations and desires to the surface. Many epics narrate the story of warrior heroes who went on the mission to slay demons and monsters. They all metaphorically indicate the state of an individual who has experienced the inner transformation and are ready to explore the unmanifest consciousness of the Universe. Agni is used in every ritual in Hindu religions. It becomes a witness at the time of marriage. It also becomes the funeral pyre when the physical body is consumed.

Basil leaf is offered at Vishnu temples and then distributed to the devotees. It is known as Tulsi in India. The story of Tulsi refers to the power of chastity. Tulsi was an extremely devout wife. The power of her devotion made her husband invincible. He became so powerful that nothing could destroy him. The Demigods tried in vain to defeat him and did not succeed. They went to the Lords Shiva and Vishnu to help defeat this demon. Even the Lords could not destroy him because of the power of his wife's devotion. There was only one way to break this deadlock. Lord Vishnu took the form of Tulsi's husband and deceived her. She lost her chastity as a result and her husband was killed. When she realized that she had been violated, Tulsi cursed Lord Vishnu to turn into a stone (Saligram). Later on she forgave Lord Vishnu who blessed her to be worshipped by all for her chastity. Tulsi leaves are offered at every Vishnu temple. A plant is always present at the Vishnu temples. A ritualistic marriage ceremony is performed (Tulsi Vivah) at the end of the monsoon season. It also corresponds to the wedding season for Hindus. Saligram stone is found in the Himalayas. It is a fossil stone (ammonite). Ritualistic prayers are offered to this stone.

Likewise at Shiva temples, Bilva or Vilva trees (Aegle Mermelos) and leaves are used for rituals. It is also known as the golden apple tree. It has three leaves at each stem, representing the three eyes of Shiva. Vilva tree is worshipped as an embodiment of Shiva himself. In Buddhism, the Bodhi tree is similarly revered because Buddha attained enlightenment under one such tree.

Shiva worshippers also wear stripes of ash on their foreheads and bodies at various places. At the street level, people pay more attention to identifying themselves as Shaivetes or Vaishnavetes or Shakti worshippers. When under the influence of the lower Chakras, this tendency is normal. People tend to cover themselves with layers and layers of identity. The underlying reason for observing practices specific to each deity is because transcendence at the subtle level can be accomplished by different means. The combination of specific elements to achieve this transcendence varies from one system to another.

Buddhists focus more on the fire chakra (Manipuraka). Their monks wear ochre colored robes. They use mandalas, chakra sounds, meditation methods etc. directly without needing all the symbolic representations. Buddhism negates all symbolic worship. However, Hindu systems place their emphasis on indirect to direct transition in inner experience. For example, when we consume food, we really do not pay attention to what the ingredients do. We go for the smell, taste and delicacy of what we eat or drink. After that we do not worry about what it does and how our body digests it with the right combination of acids, enzymes and how the nutrients are extracted from it and then transformed into energy. That knowledge becomes important only when someone eats something that can be harmful. In general, food for consumption is well known and its benefits are very many. The cow does not know how it converts the grass it eats into nourishing milk and meat. Likewise, consumption of spiritual elements through the life processes of rituals, beliefs, devotion, festivals and functions lead to a digestion of these elements and trigger an inner spiritual transformation and growth. It is always great to know what everything does. But it is not a necessary condition. One does not have to know every part in a car and how it works, in order to drive it. The same goes for spiritual process starting from a religious education.

All the drama of romance, love, marriage, emotions, rituals, gifts, celebrations, anniversaries, flowers, greeting cards, gifts etc. are meant only for one fundamental purpose - reproduction. We spend more time on the process that leads to the outcome rather than directly going to it. This is because the process subliminally involves finding the matching likes and vibrations for two individuals to get close to each other. How two people connect to each other is not measurable or predictable. It happens through introduction, interaction, familiarity, likes and dislikes that lead to subsequent steps. All these happen in the mind before the bodies come closer. Everything is done through a process of drama because that is how the mind accepts anything and learns from it. Things become real only through inner experience. Until then it is only heard from someone or read or imagined.

What seem to be important are the conditions and environment that are conducive for spiritual nucleation and growth. Living organisms did not get dropped at various places on this earth. All that happened was the emergence of an environment that would support and sustain life forms. The necessary ingredients might have been there on the earth itself or brought from outside. The combination of the two helped life forms to emerge and be sustained by the environment. The Hindu systems have done the same thing. Emphasis has been placed on the conditions and environment. Then the rest will take care of itself. The purpose is not to make everyone progress at the same time, at the same rate. Instead, progress happens by sporadic nucleation, followed by growth. Nucleation happened through masters arising at various places at various times and simply adding to the existing system. Even if what they founded appeared somewhat different from the norm, over time, everything got assimilated into the system. Assimilation process happened slowly over time so that various systems already present could begin to interconnect with the new one.

Modern India has made everything just a symbolic act. There is no time to really understand all the subtle meanings of everything that is being done according to tradition. Package deals, shorter versions, ready-made ritual items etc. have become a commercial reality. Cost of sustaining a staff at the temples has gone up. In some temples, the traditional instrument players have disappeared and in their place, pre-recorded play back systems are being used. A generation ago, things were a little slower. A few generations ago, people would not move a step forward without observing the traditional practices. Almost everyone in my grandfather's generation wore their religious symbols on their foreheads, bathed without fail in the morning and the evening, referred to the astrological charts, learned the ritual practices and scriptures and did not miss any of them. The real India has withdrawn from the surface with more commercialization and modernization. However, everything is cyclical in nature. With the advent of the Internet, many are able to find references much easier and an interest is resurging. Yoga and Pranayama which had been an esoteric practice in India, gained popularity in the Western world and now there is a lot of interest in India as a result. There is a lot more knowledge available at the click of a button on the computer. Temples are mushrooming in many places. Many are being built without the knowledge of what the temples are meant for and why their construction process is critical. Temples were built in the past using a code that was not written down.

19 THE TEMPLE

The traditional Hindu temple is built based on a code known as the Agama Shastra. "Agama" simply means tradition. Temples were built to absorb cosmic energy so that a devotee could step in and absorb it by simply being there. To accomplish this task, temples were built based on certain geometric patterns. Their deities faced certain directions based on the geographical location. The foundation process, the civil engineering involved, the soil, the deity, the features of the deity etc. were very specific. Some of these aspects are still followed. In Southern India, many kings and emperors prided themselves in building massive temples. Based on the patronage for a particular sect, the corresponding temple was built. Shiva temples outnumber all the others in Southern States.

Temples became centers for culture and tradition. There were temples built for different purposes – bringing wealth, improving health, blessing for children, for overcoming distress and so on. In some temples, traditional practices have been in vogue for more than a thousand years. Until about a century ago, temples boasted dance halls, elephants, cows, lands and orchards. There were dedicated women dancers in each temple. They were simply married off to the deity of the temple and danced in temple functions. They were called as "Deva Dasi" (Lord's follower). The Deva Dasis nurtured the tradition of music, dance and drama that was passed on from mother to daughter. Like any system, it slowly got corrupted and the term "Deva Dasi" came to mean a prostitute. Over the years, the temple dancers have disappeared. Respectable people have taken up their dance tradition and now it is taught to many.

Many temples have lost the patronage that they had been receiving. Independent India underwent its own transformation. Many people sustaining these temples, left to work elsewhere in the government and private sector industry where monetary gains were much better. Many belonging to the priest community began to migrate to big metros and integrated into the modern world. For some time, the priests suffered from extreme poverty. Government and private grants have begun to make this profession somewhat lucrative. The original purpose of the temples seems to have been forgotten. Many additions have been made, reconstruction carried out and commercialization and tourism have added to the reality more. Now these temples stand out for their grand architecture and sculpture. People still come to temples to get Divine blessings. But most come for mundane requests for making their daily lives better. That is how it has been. Amongst the many, one can arise and nucleate the awareness within.

The important step one has to take inside a temple is to simply sit on the floor for sometime. If the temple still can retain the cosmic energy in it, then it will charge the person who would simply sit on the floor anywhere inside the temple. It is important to remain grounded with the root chakra connected to the earth. This is the main reason why one is required to walk barefoot inside Hindu temples. Men are not allowed to wear upper garments in certain orthodox temples even now. A generation ago and before, men seldom wore any upper garments in Southern India. They smeared their skin with sandalwood paste and wore their religious symbols on their foreheads without fail. Bathing in a river or the temple pond was a daily routine.

Not only the temple, but also the streets leading to the temple, the homes and surroundings were maintained with this devotional spirit in the past. One walks around the temple clockwise. Each temple had four entrances, representing the four directions. Once a devotee goes around the temple outside, he enters the temple from the front entrance. There are courtyards and long passages that he went through in a clockwise direction again. Some people would roll their bodies along the corridors. Along these long corridors, there would be smaller temples for many other deities and saints. The important factor here is not only being in the temple, but also having the faith and devotion. If there is no belief, then it cuts off any effect on a person. Emotions are extremely critical in order to derive the maximum benefit of being inside a temple.

India is full of holy places. Some are very famous and have a history based on mythology or beliefs. Some are extremely remote and sometimes inaccessible. Pilgrimage is a strong tradition. Sometimes people would offer to travel all the way by foot to a pilgrimage site. In the past, that was the only mode of transportation. Nowadays there are cars, vans, buses, trains and flights. A pilgrim would typically observe some kind of penance over a period of time until the completion of the pilgrimage. The rivers in India are considered to be holy, just like the temples. Most have female names in Sanskrit. The confluence of holy rivers takes a spiritual dimension. Famous temples and pilgrimage sites exist at the confluence of these rivers. A flowing river represents life current. Her energy sustains life around her banks. Rivers correspond to Nadis in the human. There are Nadis named after some of the rivers that flow in India. The confluence of Nadis in the ethereal body corresponds to the confluence of the terrestrial rivers. On specific auspicious occasions, spiritually minded people converge at the river confluences to take a dip at a chosen astrological time. This has been going on for thousands of years. The most famous one of these is the Kumbh Mela (Festival of the Pot). It is the largest gathering of human beings on the planet for a religious occasion. Many advanced yogis and gurus descend from the high mountains to attend the Kumbh Mela. Being there itself is considered adequate to absorb the spiritual energy in the place.

Not just rivers, sometimes cremation grounds are revered as well. The holy city of Benares has its cremation grounds where many aspire to get cremated when they die. If they get cremated there, the belief is that rebirth is not needed. Benares is the abode of Lord Shiva who is known as the Lord of Death. He resides at the cremation ground. Many yogis meditate at the funeral sites. They smear the funeral ash on their skin. Benares is home to many advanced yogis and gurus.

A yogi avoids visiting temples. A fully renounced yogi is known as a Sanyasin. Typically a funeral rite is performed in the presence of a master and all bonds at that point are broken. A wandering Sanyasi has no family. His name is changed. A yogi considers his whole body as the temple. Therefore there is no need to visit any temple.

20 THE YOGI

A yogi is one who is in pursuit of Yog or union. This union happens at the spiritual level. He uses the body as the temple and vehicle to attain the state of Super consciousness. The yogic tradition in India is very old. No one knows when it started. Yogis are there all across India. Yet coming across a real yogi is not an easy task. Many avoid being in public and stay focused on their single-minded pursuit of Divine Union.

Yogis are highly revered and respected in India. A fully renounced Sanyasin (another word for a yogi) carries no belongings, has no attachment to any place and keeps away from worldly affairs. Aspiring yogis seek the guidance of an accomplished master, serving him and being under his guidance at all times. They revere their master like God and would not cross the line their master draws. Being accepted by a master is no easy task. An accomplished master really wants to see an unquenchable thirst in a seeker for realizing the Divine experience within. Only then guidance comes.

Typically yogis wear white or ochre colored clothing. Trimming hair is discouraged. Many yogis let their facial hair grow and have long hair that they roll up and twine. According to tradition, natural hair, and uncut and untrimmed serves as antenna for cosmic energy. Yogis curl up the hair to energize their crown Chakra using their long hair as antennae. The hair is periodically washed and maintained in order to preserve its vitality in drawing cosmic energy.

Many accomplished yogis also wear minimal clothing and some go simply naked. This is also done to maximize the entry of Prana, or life-current into the body through maximum exposure. There are several orders or systems of lineage for yogis. Some follow the path of Shiva. Some follow Vishnu. Those who follow the methods of Tantra follow Shakti. Yogis come in many shades. Some look very benign and welcoming. Some look terrifying and frightening. Depending upon which system they follow, their outward appearance reflects that order. However, yogis in general are very benevolent beings. They use different methods to dissuade public from interfering with their daily activities. Some withdraw into deep jungles and mountain caves. Some keep moving from place to place.

A yogi begs for alms. In receiving the alms, a powerful yogi is known to lessen or eliminate Karmic debts in people. This story is repeated many times over across the land. If a yogi appears at the doorstep asking for food, people generally do not refuse. They offer whatever food they have and the yogi quietly accepts it and walks away. In that process, one believes the removal of some Karma. There are many quacks that also masquerade as yogis and demand food from people. That is an unfortunate reality.

The yogis developed the science of yoga and Pranayama. Many practice these techniques to hone their physical as well as astral bodies, removing blockages to the flow of life force, its manipulation to achieve higher spiritual experience and using advanced methods to sustain the body under extreme conditions. Some yogis are known to go without food or water for days while spending all the time on deep meditation. Yogis arise from the general population. The process by which they reached this stage is through what I have explained in the prior chapters – being continuously exposed to the Divine elements in the surrounding, developing an awareness through life's experience, seeking more of it and finally becoming ready. This does not happen in one lifetime. That is the belief in all Hindu religious systems. One is born many times to learn and cleanse. What is learned in each life cycle accumulates. At some

point, one becomes ready to learn the higher ideals. Until that happens, one keeps going through many life cycles.

A book named Yoga Sutra by a sage named Patanjali describes in detail all the steps one takes to become a fully realized being. A yogi's goal is to experience life to the fullest. This means he directs his conscious mind to be in the present at all times, fully aware, in control of all senses and emotions. A yogi develops full control over all his body and mind. An accomplished yogi is known to have complete control over his autonomous nervous system itself. Paul Brunton, in his book describes about a yogi who demonstrates the complete stopping of his heart and pulse by simply willing[4]. An accomplished yogi is able to remain alive even after halting his heart from beating and stopping his breath completely. This is not a stunt action.

Complete stillness is one of the steps needed to transcend to the ultimate level of spiritual experience. Through the practice of Pranayama and yoga, as well as through proper guidance, a yogi is able to open up all his Nadis and cleanse his Chakras. At this stage, he is ready to receive the blissful experience of Divine realization. A guru usually triggers this experience either by being physically present in the vicinity or sometimes by simply willing it remotely. When the trigger happens, the Sushumna Nadi opens its path for Kundalini at the root Chakra to ascend upwards. The yogi has undergone proper preparation under guidance to withstand any new experience and simply accepts it as the Kundalini ascends. Generally a guru's blessing is needed for Kundalini to reach the highest Chakra above the crown of the yogi's head. When the union of Shakti and Shiva happens at the crown Chakra, the yogi is fully liberated. He has transcended mortal death. His consciousness now expands beyond his body and spreads in all directions. He is filled with unconditional love towards everything. At this stage, the yogi has become one with the Universe. This is known as the super conscious state, which is called as virgin birth.

A yogi has the choice to leave his mortal body and remain in complete awareness of the Universe (The state of Brahma). He can leave his body at will. However, many yogis decide to stay and guide others to reach their Divine realization. Such yogis direct their Kundalini to their heart Chakra and she remains there for them. In ordinary mortals, Kundalini resides at the root Chakra, near the base of the spine. When we look outward, deriving our experience through the senses, Kundalini becomes ego. When turned inwards, withdrawing the senses, ego is suppressed. When Kundalini if fully united with the Universal Consciousness at the crown Chakra, one's ego is completely crushed. It is known by many names in other cultures as well. For example, in Islamic religion it is called as the killing of the infidel. If ego is not destroyed, it can return and take over the mind of an accomplished yogi, leading to his own self-destruction. The story of the lion at the beginning of this book gives an example of it.

Many anthologies collected over centuries, have described the experience of Divine Union or the Kundalini experience. Yogis have sung them in complete ecstasy. Some take the form of romantic love. Some are in the form of describing the Divine mother. A fully realized yogi can sense the astral body in others. It is the realized yogis who have brought the knowledge of Chakras, their characteristics, the Nadis, the various practices to cleanse and activate them. The system of Chakras and Nadis did not originate from one single individual and taken as a truth. It became an accepted tradition when many experienced the same symptoms and understood what they meant on their own and shared that knowledge with others. A yogi attains full control not only over his physical body, but also over the astral body, consisting of four layers (etheric, mental, emotional and spiritual). He can expand his astral body to connect with that of others. When such a connection happens, the other person undergoes a blissful experience as well. However, the yogi knows that everyone must be ready to receive.

When yogis leave their bodies (it is not mentioned as death), in general, they are not cremated. They are buried in a seated position with their legs crossed, inside a pit and the pit is filled with a variety of items like salt, rice, oil etc. Then the pit is closed. Usually a tree is planted at the burial place or a small temple is erected. The yogi is not considered dead. His spirit is full of awareness and is believed to

bless those who visit the burial place. People pray to trees in India. In many places these trees were planted at the burial places of yogis.

Many yogis retreat to the mountains and caves to spend their time in meditation. Most yogis prefer to be in bliss and nothing else. They seldom come into the masses. Even if they do, they keep a very low profile and minimal interaction. Only if they desire to help others, do they spend their time with ordinary humans. Sometimes they respond to the prayers of spiritual seekers who are looking for guidance.

Since they achieve expanding their awareness and will power beyond their bodies, they can transcend the death of the mortal body. They can now continue to be alive even after the body has been discarded. A yogi therefore has no fear of death. His experience of bliss is reached through the stillness of his body and mind, which resembles the state of physical death. In Sanskrit, this state is known as Samadhi (Sama means balance). A yogi entering Samadhi enters this state by slowing down his breath and heartbeat and almost bringing it to a halt. In that state, they experience a blissful state that has been described in many ways. A yogi can stay in this condition for 21 days. Achieving the state of Samadhi is the ultimate experience in one's spiritual development. Though this sounds easy, it takes a lifetime of effort and as the belief goes, many lifetimes as well. The yogi develops tremendous psychic and intuitive power by experiencing Samadhi. These powers have been mentioned in many works including the Yoga Sutra by Patanjali. However, a fully realized yogi who has crushed his entire ego has no interest in those powers. He does use them sometimes to help an aspiring seeker or guide his followers.

There are many fantastic stories about yogis and advanced masters known as Siddhas. Knowing about them becomes a part of the growing up in the region. Sometimes a child would suddenly assume a yogic posture and go into deep meditation. People would flock to see the child seated like a yogi and in complete stillness.

Deep meditation is not the simple closing of the eyes and sitting in a cross-legged position. When someone goes into such deep meditation it is usually in the Samadhi state. Anyone who has achieved this state has no interest whatsoever in the materialistic benefits of the world. They become childlike in their inner purity. They have complete control over all their body organs and mind.

A yogi is also known to leave his body at will by letting his exit happen through the crown Chakra. This has been mentioned to me many times and is well known across the land. It would be mentioned as Maha Samadhi (The Great Samadhi) [5]. The yogi permanently leaves the body and it is buried or cremated after the exit. Some yogis exit their old bodies and enter the dead bodies of the young. This has been mentioned as Parakaya Pravesha. Instead of taking birth in another body and going through all the learning stages, some yogis are said to avoid this process by simply discarding their aging bodies and finding bodies of those who died young. Through the power of intuition, a yogi can sense the demise of someone young and can decide to enter the dead body with all the full consciousness and spiritual advancement[6].

Yogis do things differently. Yogic breathing is very deep. The inhalation and exhalation cycles are extremely long. A yogi can completely slow the breath down to a halt. Yogananda says, "Breathless is Deathless." The yogic sleep is also interesting. It is known as Yoga Nidra where his body and mind sleep while he can be fully aware and awake. By extending this experience, he is able to retain the same awareness by experiencing death in his body and keeping himself alive in the process. Swami Rama mentions that the knowledge of life exists in knowing the secret of death[7]. Transcending death leads to immortal life. Living is simply the process of being conscious and aware. Whether one can do it using a body or out of it is immaterial. A yogi learns to use his body and mind to reach the state where he can retain his living experience even without his body. The union of Kundalini with the Universal consciousness at the crown Chakra results in a deathlike stillness in the body and mind. However, one who has undergone this awakening is still alive and simply does not want anything else from this world after this experience.

Shiva is depicted as a yogi. This is because He is associated with death. He is the Lord of Death and dissolution. He meditates in the cremation ground. All these are symbolic representation of what a yogi experiences by transcending the state of death with full awareness. This implies there is no such thing as death if one can experience it. Experience can happen only through the process of living. Therefore if one can experience death and beyond, he is still alive. Like a headache, one has to experience it for himself and it cannot be described in words or by any other means. Every inner experience has to be experienced in order to know what it means.

If one were to ask me whether I have seen any demonstration of what I am describing here, my answer is no. I am only mentioning what I have heard from others and from what I have read. However these aspects of yogis have been mentioned at many places in the history of the land. Even if I were to encounter a fully accomplished yogi, he is going to have no desire to show off his prowess to me. He has no ego and therefore no urge to demonstrate those powers. Most demonstrations are done by half-baked quacks that seek attention and following. Sometimes they have failed in their demonstrations and have strengthened the doubts in others about these powers. The only way to know if these powers are true is to become a yogi oneself. If one did that he is not going to run back to others to confirm what he found. When one becomes an accomplished yogi, there is no going back. His doubts are removed and he has no further interest in announcing his achievement to anyone. Therefore what I have mentioned here is purely something that is a part of the belief system across the land.

A yogi is fully aware at every instant of experience. He can convert every experience into bliss. Duality simply disappears for an accomplished yogi. An inner balance arises and he treats the extremes of duality with equal poise.

21 THE BODY AS THE TEMPLE

Yogis brought the truth about the body itself being a temple where Divinity resides. We all know the physical body. We also do not know much about it. We leave that responsibility with the doctors. We all know we exist in our bodies and the outward appearance is what we interact with most of the time. We do not pay much attention to what our bodies do or how we are abusing them. Our attention happens only when the body falls sick or we get hurt. Otherwise we do not feel like maintaining it well. Somehow we feel eternal. Most of us do not think about the mortal end to our bodies. We see others die, but somehow we do not think about the day when we would be there too.

Most people do not even pay attention to their breathing. "Normal" people breathe abnormally. We eat and enjoy the taste. After that we do not care much about how the body processes it. We crave and over indulge. Many smoke tobacco products, drink too much alcohol and abuse their internal systems even more. With mind under duress it causes more internal damage to the physical body. We have doctors for that, don't we? But we do not like to follow doctor's recommendations much. May be we would do it for a short while and then abandon them. We need medication that simply heals us and we do not want to think about it much. Welcome to the modern world.

The first task for a spiritual seeker is to have a healthy body. Without a healthy body, spiritual pursuit will be hard to keep up.

Physical health is essential for mental health. Abuse of the body leads to mind damage. This leads one towards the darkness of ignorance. One begins to lose human qualities and tends towards simple animal like existence. A healthy body is not sustained by physical exercise alone. Mind and body have to be exercised together. A holistic approach is needed in improving the overall health. Excluding the mind and focusing on the body can cause more harm. Without making the body healthy, mind will not get healthier.

People who lived a few centuries ago were luckier than we are today when seen from a spiritual standpoint. This is because they had to rely on natural resources for their livelihood. Life was not fast paced. There were fewer people. There were more abundant resources. Contamination and pollution of natural resources were absent. Under those conditions, the body and mind in people were much healthier to make spiritual progress compared to today.

Those who made advanced strides in spiritual progress realized the importance of mind-body interdependence and their health. They also realized that the mind-body system was not entirely physical. They sensed subtler layers that could not be realized through the sensory organs. They realized that amongst all the steps to be taken, breath was the first step. In any spiritual practice in India, breathing exercises are taught first. This happened through a ritual called "Upanayanam" where a disciple is ceremoniously sent off with a teacher who teaches him Gayathri Mantra and breathing exercises. It has become a symbolic act today. In the past it was done quite seriously. A male child left his parents at the age of six to be with his master in learning the skills to support life and returned by the age of 18 to be married. During those twelve years, he learned many spiritual practices and ritualistic procedures thoroughly.

Breath is the most fundamental aspect of our existence. From the time a child comes out of the womb crying to the very end, breath and heartbeat go on continuously. One can remain without food or liquid for a few hours to few days. An ordinary mortal cannot survive without breath for more than a few minutes. Proper breathing is the first step towards mind-body health. In an abused mind-body system like we all have today, breath follows the mind. If the mind wanders off in all directions, breath becomes shallow. We seldom fill our lungs with fresh air to capacity. We seldom breathe out completely. When capacity is not filled, they call it an inefficient system in science. The mind becomes restless, wanders in all directions, getting anxious, stressed, worried, hurt and tense causing health issues in the body as one grows and ages. Life has become so busy now that people do not have the time to sit and breathe right for a few minutes. Sitting with a quiet mind seems almost impossible.

Yogis realized the importance of breath in spiritual progress. For advancement in spiritual quest, one has to reverse the unnatural process of breath following the mind. If mind follows the breath, it reverses everything. If the breath slows, so does the mind. If one focused on the breath, the mind becomes steadier. A steady mind is not fluttering about worrying, feeling anxious, angry and stressed. It begins to resemble still water where reflections appear mirror like. Many breathing techniques have been developed by yogis for various effects.

It is not adequate if one did proper breathing and other exercises. It is also important to develop one's character and observe strict discipline. In Sanskrit these are called as Yama and Niyama. By avoiding wrong deeds and choices, by observing fasts, and cleansing methods, one learns to condition the body and mind towards spiritual pursuit. If one wants to lose weight and maintain a healthy body, discipline has to be exercised in diet and follow certain exercises to train the mind to avoid craving. Yama and Niyama are similar for training the mind and body towards spiritual pursuit.

The food one consumes has a significant impact on a person's inner character. Once a spiritual seeker has become serious on his pursuit, he has to pay attention to what he consumes. Meat is avoided for the initiates because it has elements that can affect the subtle Nadis and induce what is known as Tamasic tendencies (towards more worldly, materialistic desires). There are traditions in Tantra where the trainees consume tobacco, alcohol and meat. But it is done in a controlled manner under the guidance of an adept, after achieving a certain degree of control over body and mind. This is more of an esoteric practice compared to the other paths. Food intake is minimized slowly. A spiritual aspirant takes fewer meals each day. By training the body and mind to demand less food, one develops will power.

Reliance on nature is emphasized. At this stage, one starts wandering in search of spiritual experience. Bathing in running water like rivers and streams is encouraged. This is also the stage when yogic exercises are started. There are hundreds of yogic postures. Based on one's constitution, the appropriate exercises are taught under the guidance of a master. Sometimes finding the right master is a monumental task. All these exercises are directed towards purging oneself and clearing blockages of Nadis and tuning the Chakras.

Once breath has been stabilized, there are more practices to steady the mind. One of them is eye fixation (TrAtaka). Eye follows the mind. By steadying the eye, mind can become fixed. By physically fixing the eyes at one spot or gazing at something steadily, eye wandering is reduced. This in turn begins to steady the mind. Wandering mind disrupts the meditative process, be it static or physical activity.

Practices are combined with mantra chanting and in some systems, offering selfless service to others. These exercises help purify the Chakras. The human body is not just made up of physical elements alone, according to the advanced Hindu spiritual system. The body has an Astral component which is made up of different layers (Kosha) – etheric, mental, emotional and Spiritual. Self realized yogis have mentioned about sensing these layers through individual experiences. Knowledge about the spiritual layers, presence of Nadis or meridians, Chakras or channels, presence of different consciousness planes (or worlds), Kundalini etc. have been developed through the individual experience of many yogis across the land. Even the syllables and symbols one sees in Sanskrit have been developed entirely by the sages in the sub-continent during deep meditation. These syllables carry vibrations that can help cleanse a person from within.

The yogic system sees the body as being connected to the Universe. There are elements in the body that correspond to those in the Universe. The way to establish connectivity through spiritual process is to train the body and mind to tune into it. Therefore by using one's body, one can establish the connectivity to the Universe. The spinal column plays the central part in the yogic system. It is not even the brain. The spine is extremely important. An erect stance is always emphasized for meditation. Posture (Asana) is extremely important in yoga to achieve spiritual progress.

The whole body thus is treated like a temple and the worship happens in pure meditation. The worship here has a very deep meaning. In general when we think of the word worship, we associate it with folding both hands in respect or kneeling down in front of a deity, closing the eyes and asking for favors. That is the street level view of worship. In yogic view, worship means complete identification with what is being focused on. There is no subject and object. Both become merged. The experience that results is pure worship. We are doing this and are not paying attention to it. We are entirely identified with our bodies. It runs our life. And whatever we experience is not apart from us. It is merged with our bodily selves.

In the case of our bodies, our experience is entirely subjective and there is no objective view of it. Or one can say the two are merged. In that process, we are worshipping our life experience in us. When that worship stops, our mortal bodies die. A fully accomplished yogi merges himself with the Universal Consciousness. In crude terms we call it God. Every experience for a yogi is Universal. His will has merged with Universal will. By entering the temple of his body, a yogi manages to connect to the Universal Consciousness and merge with it. This is called by many names across the world. In the Hindu systems, there are many names to it as well – Kundalini experience, Union of Shiva and Shakti, Viswa Roopa (Universal vision), Samadhi etc.

Every breath is prayer in itself. If one breathed properly, paying attention to inhalation and exhalation, filling the lungs to full capacity and exhaling completely, he is reciting the syllables Va (inhalation) and Shi (Exhalation). When repeated, the syllables become VaShiVa, ShiVa and Shiva. Shiva is the breath that even an atheist is reciting unknowingly. It is a prayer that is recited in a cacophonic way by everyone as their breaths become shallow and their minds wander. But it is still a noisy prayer. If one did the breath consciously and properly, then the syllables take life and health of the body and mind improve tremendously. ShiVa is the breath mantra that is recited from the time one emerges from the womb till the time he is carried off for cremation or burial. It is traditional to mention one's passing away as "He breathed his last." Breath is the last one to stop.

All temples have drums being played during rituals. Certain drum sounds correspond to a chakra. Shiva is depicted with a drum on His hand. Every Chakra is associated with an astral sound that a yogi hears internally during deep meditation. Normal people, when sitting in silence can hear the astral sound of the root Chakra, which sounds like a honeybee. Sometimes when a deafening sound happens, the ears return to the senses again after a deep, high pitch sound is heard internally. During the first stage of meditation, this sound can be heard very clearly. Likewise, the Sacral Chakra has a flute like astral sound associated with it. This is also the chakra for romance and reproduction. Krishna, the Hindu God for romance is depicted with a flute on his hands. The navel chakra is associated with a string instrument like astral sound. The heart chakra when stimulated creates an astral sound resembling bells. Throat chakra creates an astral sound that resembles the thundering roar of a waterfall or the ocean waves[7]. When Kundalini passes through the Sushumna Nadi, she crosses the different Chakras and a person experiencing her passage will hear these various sounds. Similarly, a yogi will experience various astral smells. These resemble camphor, incense, flower essence smells.

In many Hindu temples, these sounds and smells are an integral part of daily rituals. Since the human body is a temple with all these internal sensations, the same stimulant sensations have been set up in Hindu temples. A Hindu temple is constructed to resemble a body with the astral different layers (Kosha). The deity in the sanctum is the spiritual body (Anandamaya Kosha) while the street is the starting point or Physical body (Annamaya Kosha). A Brahman, who is self realized, connects his inner self to the cosmic consciousness by penetrating the spiritual body. No one else can enter the inner sanctum unless they have prepared themselves and practiced all the spiritual exercises to reach that far. In the Hindu temples, the Brahman priests (who are not really self realized Brahmans in the real sense) have taken the privilege of being allowed into the inner sanctum of the Hindu temples. Someone has to offer prayers and perform rituals to the inner deity. Therefore, the Brahman community has been given the sanction to enter the sanctum. The Brahmans who have this qualification are expected to observe all codes mentioned in the scriptures, be pious and orthodox, and know the various scriptures and ritual practices.

Every body therefore is a temple, an abode of the Divinity, however corrupt one might be. All the appearance of absolute evilness is only a layer surrounding the pure spirit. Karma is meant for washing away these layers. This belief is strongly enforced in most Hindu systems. When one greets another, they always bring both palms together, offering prayer to the soul in the other person. The average person does not think about it and such a greeting is now confined mostly to functions. People are westernized nowadays and prefer to shake hands.

The purpose of Hindu religious systems has been to build that awareness in each individual about the realization that the body is a temple of the Universe. Each body is connected to the Universe and can realize this connectedness in a single lifetime if one so desires. Everything is based on the spiritual layers of the Astral body, the physical body, the Nadis, the Chakras, realizing their significance through the drama of life, karma and guidance.

Every body does feel individualistic. Living experience in the body is limited. We tend to think that we live only inside our bodies. In a sense driven perspective that is outward looking, that idea is all right. Every fish that swims in the ocean is individualistic. Each can move about in its own independent way. Each one can make its own decisions on where to go and what to do. The fish cannot exist without its body. Nor can it exist without the water in which it lives. It lives not only in the body, as well as in the water that surrounds it.

When a being cannot live without something, then that something may be external to the body, but it becomes a part of the body. And the body becomes a part of it. One cannot think of itself apart from what supports their lives. We live on this planet, having evolved under its gravitational field, fully used to the atmospheric pressure at its surface, breathing the air, being protected by the atmosphere, being sustained by the water that surrounds the earth's surface, relying on the energy from the sun to remain warm and consume food that is dependent on the sun's energy, the seasons that go with it and the gravitational force of the moon which affects the whole circadian rhythm. All of it becomes a part of our individual bodies because we cannot survive without them. Individuality is simply a thin membrane that provides a shape to our bodies. A yogi, in self-realization, experiences the wholeness of his being and his body now expands to include everything that surrounds it and sustains it.

Looking outward, relying entirely on one's senses, one needs religions, scriptures, rules, codes and social activities. We need to be guided. When one begins to look inward, one begins to understand the origin of all the societal codes, morals, rules, scriptures and religions. In that process, one goes beyond religion. Shiva is associated with the mountain (Himalayas). At the bottom of the mountain, there are many pathways and trails that lead towards the top. As the elevation changes, the paths begin to merge and at the summit all paths have merged. This is the principle of the mountain. The ascent to the summit starts with many routes. Religions are like the different pathways. Many do not realize the presence of a summit. The mountain is so huge that it gives the deceptive appearance where there is no awareness of something called the summit. Going up there seems difficult. So many prefer to stay down below where their needs are met. Those who have reached the summit seldom want to come back down and out of those some have returned to tell them about what is up at the summit and it makes no sense to those who are still at the starting trails.

Beyond the timberline of spiritual transformation, the desire to reach the summit increases. Reaching the timberline seems monumental to many. Religions are the bridge between the physical world and the spiritual realm. The journey happens inwards and not the other way around.

Buddha decided to do away with the drama of life and all the ritualistic, indirect methods to induce spiritual desires in people. He decreed that any desire leads to suffering. During his time, his method was justifiable. The whole system had been corrupted and exploitation and manipulation of others using privileges due to religious hierarchy was the norm. Buddha decided to go directly to the path of Chakras, Nadis and Astral bodies and using the body as the vehicle. There was no need for Avatars and Gods in that system. He did not even utter the word God. He maintained silence when asked about it. What has to be experienced cannot be explained, and especially to those who are at the kindergarten level of spirituality.

However, most humans, who are like children from a spiritual standpoint, do not have the means to know and understand all the principles directly. Everything has to be allegorical and metaphorical. When little children are taught the basics, they are taught in ways that they can relate to – by playing, singing, having recess, sleep times and so on. Everything is taught through the theme of plays and games. That is how most humans are from a spiritual standpoint. In the long run, the Hindu systems returned to dominance in India because of this appeal for the people who are spiritually childlike. Even Buddhism has splintered into four schools and beyond. In some places, people simply pray to the statue of sleeping Buddha seeking favors. It is the natural tendency in humans to seek favors from a higher being. We are wired that way.

The purpose here is not to make everyone enlightened in one swoop. That is impossible. Many masters have come and tried to help people around experience enlightenment. However, only a handful of them really managed to reach those levels. The others were impressed and became loyal followers. A few generations later, they divided and began to fight each other. This has been the case in every system. Everyone is not meant to reach the same level of enlightenment at the same time.

We have to see what everything around us is teaching. In nature everything around has a message. If one were to be spiritual and advance in it, he or she has to sense this message in everything around. The tree, the river, the mountains, the ocean, the clouds, the rain, the sunlight, the cosmos, and the ground – everything has a hidden message. Only the ones who are sensitive enough to pick up those messages benefit from them. This is much like a rocky landscape where everyone poses for photographs. But if there was a geologist, he is going to look at the whole thing differently. His training and experience will trigger his senses and he would be looking at the rocks and extracting information from them. He might think about how old these rocks are, what those intrusions are, what the texture is, what kind of minerals they contain and so on. He would admire something totally different from all the other tourists around. To him the place becomes an information trove that helps him read into the distant past and help reconstruct a history of the land that is hidden in those rocks.

A spiritual seeker is much like the geologist. He is sensing all the hidden messages and teachings from everything around him. If an environment is set up to give that information, it will trigger more people to turn spiritual and sense those messages. The Universe is full of teaching and learning happens from within when one becomes ready on his own, at his own time. Everyone is not ready to graduate to the next level simultaneously. This is true when changes have to happen within, devoid of any coercion.

22 THE TEACHING

India is a land of great rivers, mountains, forests and animals. A spiritual seeker is able to sense the hidden messages in them and enhance his experience.

Rivers are considered holy in the Hindu religions. Almost all rivers across the land, except for one, are given feminine names. I had mentioned earlier that femininity is associated with life energy. The life energy in the human is called Kundalini. A river does not go in a straight line. She winds her way to the ocean. As she winds her way, she also sustains life within her and around her. Vegetation grows in abundance on her banks. Fish and other aquatic animals live in the river. People are able to drink the water in her and wash themselves. No matter how clean or dirty someone is, the river always cleanses him. It does not care how dirty someone is. It is in the nature of a river to cleanse and take away the dirt. Anyone getting into the river comes out cleansed and refreshed. Every being has pure spirit deep inside its inner sanctum. The experience through the drama of life can build up layers and layers of ignorance to such an extent that we call that being evil. In reality there is no such thing as evil. Just like the river cleansing away all layers of dirt, Kundalini cleanses the layers of identity and karma as she ascends towards the seat of Universal consciousness or the grand ocean.

The layers of ignorance are stored in the lower Chakras. The more they accumulate, the more drawn one becomes towards the Tamasic state of darkness. Taking a dip in a river or any running stream creates the link between the water element and the Sacral Chakra.

Cleansing of this chakra is essential for spiritual enhancement. If this chakra is purified and all the dirt in it is purged, it is like falling into the running river and coming out cleansed. The flowing river has this message. Nowadays drainage and chemicals are being dumped into rivers, turning them into sewers. But the current is still flowing at the bottom, far removed from the floating dirt on top. The grand ocean takes it all and dissolves it. Then it returns the water in the form of clouds and rain that come back through the river again. By cycling repeatedly, purification is achieved. The mortal being goes through life cycles in a similar way, returning purified and going through the drama of life again to cleanse and learn more from experience. This is a part of the spiritual journey for every individual. The one who realizes the principle is now ready to go to the next stage of learning to remain cleansed and coming out of the life cycles to merge with the cosmic ocean permanently.

The tree has a message too. Every tree is nurturing. Its branches and leaves provide the cool shade. It breathes oxygen out and our survival depends upon the vegetation on this planet. The roots hold the soil together. One can use the logs for fuel or for making furniture and build homes. One can eat the fruits. The tree not only supports humans, but also animals and birds. Trees become the world of monkeys. Birds build their nests on them. One can build a float and cross bodies of water. And the log from the tree is extremely strong and flexible. The tree symbolizes the state of Brahmacharya. A Brahmachari is a person who has complete control over his senses and remains deeply rooted and unshakeable. He is strong and yet flexible. He does not get agitated easily and does not get tempted to show off his power and strength. He remains benevolent to everyone and protects those who are weak. He fights for just causes and helps everyone in distress. A Brahmachari does not fall for sense pleasures and remains celibate in order to strengthen his spiritual powers. Nothing can tempt him.

In the Hindu mythology two such people are depicted as Brahmacharis - Hanuman, the monkey God in the grand epic Ramayana is one. In the other epic, Mahabharata, Bhishma is another example. Bhishma is the son of mother Ganga (the holy river). He remains a Brahmachari all the way to the end. He ends up fighting a grand war on the wrong side because he has to follow the Dharma (righteousness) to do the right thing in all circumstances. When a giant tree falls, the earth shakes.

The mountain has its message. It is the mountain that stops the clouds and lets rainfall over the land. Though it is based on the land, its summit touches the sky. It is the source of great rivers. It remains still and stable. A variety of vegetation and animals find their home on the slopes of the mountain. When one looks at a giant mountain, it triggers a sense of reverence in the heart. Compared to a human, it is mighty in every way. It is unmoving, stable and towering in appearance. It outlasts us. Thousands of generations of humans can come and go and the mountain has changed a little. A mountain takes the strikes of thunder and still remains unmoved. These are symbols of a yogi who remains unmoved during deep meditation and becomes immortal by merging his spirit with the Universal consciousness. Shiva is depicted as the Lord of the mountain.

The river Ganga is shown to spring from His head. The crescent moon decorates His hair. His purity is denoted by the whiteness of the snow on top of the mountain. Shiva's abode is called as Kailash that is known to exist in the ethereal mountain. The mountain is Shiva – the unmoving, unchanging, ever lasting Universal state of fundamental consciousness.

The ocean goes by many names. It takes many colors at different parts of the world based on the environment. In some places it is rough and violent. In some places it is tranquil and transparent. Yet it is the same ocean. Each wave in the ocean seems to rise above its surface temporarily and falls back. Each wave might appear separate from the other. But all waves belong to the same ocean. Islands appear distinctly apart, separated by the body of the ocean. Life species might be entirely different between two neighboring islands. Yet underneath, they are all connected by the same land. It is from the ocean all the clouds emerge, turn into rain, streams, rivers, lakes, glaciers and become part of vegetation and animals and everything returns to the ocean. It is the ocean in which living organisms began to arise. Without the ocean, the earth would be one horrible place. The ocean symbolizes the origin of everything. It represents the entire Universe from which everything has emerged and contained within.

At the physical level, almost every river originates from the mountain and reaches the grand ocean through the land. The whole process is sustained by the mechanism of clouds and vapor, which move up without coming into contact with the surface of the earth. When they do, they turn into rain. The cycle thus has two aspects – the physical aspect of originating, running and merging and the ethereal aspect of simply transforming and condensing. This cyclical nature keeps on going. Clouds keep on forming. Yet no one cloud is like another. It is the principle of cloud formation that remains.

Rivers keep on flowing. The rivers have to face barriers, rocks, vertical drops and change course sometimes. Yet the clouds are free to float. The flowing river represents living experience on the earthly plane and the floating clouds represent the recycling process where the departed go into until they are reborn. One may not believe in reincarnation and rebirth. My emphasis here is only on how it is perceived in the Hindu systems. Lord Vishnu is depicted as lying on a bed of a five-headed snake on a white cosmic ocean.

Everything returns to the ocean. Even the grand mountain that stands still and mighty, undergoes constant erosion. The rivers grind every rock into stones and pebbles and fine sand and carry the silt. Through the journey, every grain that made the mountain finds itself at the bottom of the ocean, completely leveled and pressed into layer after layer. As mountains go, new mountains emerge and the cycle continues. Compared to the lifetime of the humans, the cycles of a mountain do appear very long in duration, yet it happens. The Hindu systems call this the cosmic cycle. Even the Universe undergoes its own cyclical birth, end and rebirth. It is just that they seem infinitely large in comparison to our dimensions. What remains and drives all these cycles is the grand ocean of Universal Consciousness. Nothing that manifests can be permanent. Time is immaterial. Everything that manifests undergoes cyclical transformation.

Creation, operation and dissolution are the nature of this Universe. Creation can be instantaneous and life cycle can be short. Dissolution can be as quick. Scientists have discovered quantum particles that appear and disappear within a trillionth of a second. Though scientists might take offense at me taking an example from their hard work, I am writing about the Hindu system where it is custom to take from what is around and enhance one's spiritual knowledge. Therefore I cannot help taking something from what has been discovered. I am only interested in seeing the commonality in principles and I do not stake claim to any scientific discoveries or declare that in some ancient Hindu scripture it has been discovered already. It does not matter. The Universe has everything. It has the largest. It has the smallest. It has the lightest. It has the heaviest. It has the fastest. It has the slowest. It has the hottest. It has the coldest. It has light. It is full of darkness. It has everything one can imagine. Somewhere, in some corner of the Universe, what one imagines might be there. Such are the vastness and multitude that anything is probable. The Universe appears full of extremes. And the all-pervading Consciousness appears through all extremes.

23 BETWEEN THE EXTREMES

In our dualistic world, we have the subject and the object. Experience is divided into subjective and objective aspects. We see ourselves distinctly individualistic and apart from everything else. Duality appears very clear to us in our world vision. Heisenberg's Uncertainty Principle gets us to a point where subjective and objective experiences come very close. However, the object cannot be observed knowing both its position and its velocity. If it is at a certain location, we need something to strike and reflect from it so that we can sense its presence through the reflection. When something like a small quantity of energy strikes it, the object is moved from where it is. We can see objects in the sky either because they emit their own light or they reflect light emitted by the stars. Until that light reaches our eyes, we do not sense their presence. Reality is only known by experiencing it through our senses. However there is more reality that is beyond our senses and sometimes through the process of observation, scientific deduction and analysis, some aspects of reality beyond our senses have been discovered.

Scientific quest for knowledge and Spiritual quest for knowing seem diametrically opposite. In some ways it is true. Science goes strictly by evidence that is acceptable and verifiable. Models and hypotheses can be proposed. They will remain so until proven as facts. However, profound ideas that became accepted facts did not jump out of the sky. Those who discovered the theory of relativity, the principles of quantum physics, the evolution of species and those invented the harnessing of electricity, computational concepts etc. had those ideas emerge from their deep inner realms. They touched the same surface that artists, philosophers and spiritually advanced beings touch and realize their own truths. What they do is meditation itself where deep contemplation leads to profound creation of ideas, theories, poems, philosophical views and inventions. Everyone is venturing to the same depth in different ways. Some people compose music that is prodigious in nature. There is a spiritual dimension to all of this. One may like to appear modern and sophisticated and negate such a view. However, everything has a spiritual origin so long as one has to seek answers through contemplation.

A yogi experiences the reality in a different way. The subject and the object become merged into one. This inner experience is beyond the senses. A yogi practices the withdrawal of his senses. Ordinary mortals lack this capability. Therefore the Universe clearly appears between two extremes – Manifest / Unmanifest, Past / Future, Start / End, Positive / Negative, Male / Female, Up / Down and so on. One can simply list all the words and their antonyms to make a complete list of duality.

To transition from the world of opposites and extremes into the realm of oneness, one needs to find the gap between those extremes. Every pair of extremes has a gap. In some cases, this gap is extremely narrow and imperceptible. In some, it can be quite wide. A yogi is able to enter the gap and expand it. When the gap expands, the extremes disappear or merge. Let us examine some extremes and the gap between them.

Our breath has two directions – inhalation and exhalation. Between these two directions lies a gap. If one focuses on this gap and experiences the gap, he will notice the time for the gap increasing. He will also sense the duration of the inhalation and exhalation increasing. The whole breath cycle begins to slow down. Slow breath is one of the fundamental steps to take in a yogic path to salvation.

We dwell in the past memories all the time. We try to predict what the future will be. Every instant in life goes from the future into the past in an irreversible manner. Each such instant is a gap between the future and the past. We call it the present or the now. We seldom pay attention to the now. We are either dwelling in the past, agonizing over all the injustices done to us or get anxious about the future. The mind keeps wandering between these two extremes on a constant basis, leaving very little or no attention to the present moment. A yogi focuses entirely on the present moment. The past is just a history to him. The future is a mystery. The gap in between the future and the past is where the mind has no idea what it must do. It can go still if one focuses on the present at each instant. A yogi simply expands this gap by meditating entirely on the present. The conscious mind no longer wanders and sits in silence like the mouse depicted near the Ganesh idol.

Between night and day, there is a gap. We call it the twilight time. To a yogi this twilight time is extremely important. He will stand in hip deep water in a flowing river at the twilight time to enhance his spiritual practice. Between sleep and wakeful states there is a gap. The conscious mind is not active during this gap. If one can expand this gap, then he can reach into his astral layers, especially the mental and emotional layers. Every memory from one's entire life's experience is stored in the mental layer (Manomaya Kosha). And according to the Hindu belief systems, this layer also contains all the memories from every past life experience as well. By expanding the gap, a yogi can reach into these layers and find the karmic causes of his current experience and help mitigate their effect and redirect them. A yogi practices wakeful sleep (known as Yoga Nidra) where he lets his body and conscious mind sleep while he develops full awareness. When he achieves this capability, he is able to reach into the various layers of his Astral body and help correct himself. This self-correction helps in enhancing his spiritual progress. Some people call this an out of body experience. However, a yogi achieves complete control over this experience.

We have not paid attention to an important gap. We exist in this gap and therefore it appears insignificant to us. It is the gap between conception and death. It is known as life in a body. Before birth and after death, we exist in a different realm and we manage to enter the gap between the two extremes birth and death and live in our bodies. It seems like a long gap because we are living in it. Likewise, every gap can appear as long or even longer if one enters it. Time has no relevance. We entered this gap to work out our karmas and restore our balance according to the Hindu systems.

Extremes seem far apart and are linked by a gap. However extremes do come together though and when one utilizes the coming together of extremes that too enhances the spiritual experience. When inward and outward movements come together at the cross over point, one can enhance the spiritual experience. Inhalation and exhalation of breath come together at the end of each cycle. One can meditate on that gap. Day and night come together during twilight hours. One can meditate during that time. The Sun and the moon (Hot and cold) come together during eclipses. This time is an extremely auspicious moment for the spiritual seekers.

The union of male and female is a spiritual moment and can be used to enhance one's spiritual experience. The science of Tantra has methods to utilize this exercise for Divine realization. Even death, which separates the two extremes - existence in a body and leaving it, can be turned into a spiritual moment. When positive and negative charges meet, they bring electrical neutrality. Extremes might seem to appear apart. But they do come together. The right and left are two extremes. But they are together in our bodies. The right hand and the left hand come together in salutation to symbolize the Divinity when extremes meet.

Between wakeful state and sleep there is a gap. This gap can be entered and expanded. A yogi, through the process of meditation manages to enter this gap and become fully aware while his body sleeps. This state can be extremely deep. One who enters the gap between extremes experiences Divinity within. Hypnotists in fact use this gap all the time to induce deep trance in people and help them experience a state where their minds are extremely alert while the bodies are deeply relaxed. They can expand this gap quite wide. By helping their clients enter this gap and deepening the experience of it, hypnotists have achieved incredible states of mind where one can create complete numbness or catalepsy. They have managed to take people back down into the past and extracted information about issues that are the source of current problems. The science of hypnosis has been branded aside along with religion as an unreliable method of healing. In many ways, hypnosis resembles the stages of meditation.

Though it is taboo in the modern world to even mention about past lives, in hypnosis, past life regression is a common practice. People have cleared certain phobias in their minds by tracing the origin of the issue back to a life in the past. Whatever happens in the mind is extremely difficult to prove with quantifiable measurements. Since spirituality and religion deal with the human mind more, they too have not been recognized as valuable tools to develop harmony and peace in people. Meditation helps achieve the same goal and goes beyond hypnosis. Meditation helps achieve controlled catalepsy as well as control over the autonomous nervous system. Will power increases with increased experience in meditation. An accomplished yogi can bring catalepsy even to his heart by simply willing for it[4].

When extremes come together, it becomes a Divine moment because in that moment duality disappears completely. In Hindu religious and philosophical systems, this coming together has been alluded to in many ways. At the beginning of this book, I had narrated the story of the lion headed human who appeared and fought a powerful man at twilight time and at the entrance of his mansion. The story simply is a metaphorical reference to the extremes coming together and how the ego is crushed when one enters the gap between the extremes. Shiva is depicted as half male and half female (Ardha-Nari-Ishwara). When extremes are brought together, perfect inner balance happens. In a dualistic world, balance between two extremes achieves a meta-neutrality. When extremes balance, it means they have canceled each other's effect completely. Manifestation happens when this balance is disturbed. All atoms are neutral where the electric charges are perfectly balanced. When the neutral state of atoms is affected, energy is released or manifested in the form of light, heat etc. This is a well-known scientific fact. Light is a manifestation arising out of altering the atomic equilibrium.

From a dualistic perspective, extremes are real. However, it has to be realized that one cannot be sensed without the other. Darkness does not exist. But it seems be everywhere. Darkness is simply the absence of light. Everything by default is in darkness. If we close our eyes, we are in darkness right away. It is the same darkness that is everywhere in this universe. What we call as space is full of darkness. Space, which does not have any manifest characteristics, now is dark in color! What is the color of space? Is black really a color? Or is it the absence of light? Just like darkness, space is the absence of manifestation.

There is no such thing as cold. Coldness is the absence of heat. We can sense heat because heat radiates and we have organs that can sense heat. We only sense cold when we realize heat dissipating away. When we rely on senses then we can sense certain things only by the absence of what we can sense. We feel as though we sense that which is absent, or does not exist according to our sense-based experience. Absence of light is darkness. Absence of heat is coldness. We sense not only through our sense organs, but also through our interactions as well. We think, feel emotions and judge. We cannot point at anything in particular other than the object of observation, which evokes thoughts, emotions or judgment. What happens when thoughts are not present while we are awake? What is absence of thoughts? What happens when an observation does not evoke any emotions when we pay attention to it? We call it as a "cold" expression. Being cold here means not having any emotional reactions or sensations. That reference comes from the coldness of a dead body. A dead body does not self sustain any heat from within. It has no awareness or sensation. All this is due to the absence of self generated heat. So lack of emotions or feelings appear as cold as the expression of a dead body.

The natural tendency for the Universe is to be in neutrality and

balance. Manifestation occurs when the balance is affected. And everything tends to drift towards the direction of balance and neutrality again. One might wonder what causes that shift in balance. There is nothing from outside that causes imbalance to happen and the restoration to balance. It is the nature of the Universe. It is referred to as cosmic dance. Balance and changing stances is part of any dance. Shiva is depicted as a dancer to reflect this nature of the Universe.

A deity becomes a simple depiction of an experience or reality. Shiva has been depicted in many forms as we saw in this book. Every deity and the attributes shown are descriptions of states of inner experience. Worshipping a deity depicted in a certain way might appear primitive to many, but one has to understand what the deity depicts and what inner experience it is alluding to. If one can enter that experience when worshipping that form depicted, it become a gateway into a different dimension. It does not happen to everyone. However, there are a few who can enter that gateway.

The term "prayer" or "worship" has a crude meaning at the street level. It means offering salutation to a statue or a formless entity in obedience, fear and reverence. Most people at the street level of spirituality are believers. They have not progressed to the level of seekers. To them worshipping or praying has a simplistic meaning. In that process, there is a gain being expected. By praying to an idol or performing a ritual one expects some kind of a boon, mostly in the form of material gain. It is all right to be that way when one is a believer. We all love to see the innocence of children believing in Santa Claus and expecting gifts on Christmas for good behavior. But real prayer or worship has a different meaning.

At a deeper level, when one prays or worships, it means he cannot exist without it. Every breath we take is one such example. We chant the mantra of breath from the time we come into the world till the time we breathe our last. We cannot give up that prayer. It is fundamental to our existence in our bodies. We identify ourselves with our bodies. We have everything in ourselves to defend and protect our bodies. We give up our bodies only if we have to die. Now that is true worship. One cannot exist without it. When we identify with something, it is idol worship. We all worship our bodies. Our breaths are prayers. The two are needed for our very existence. And then we identify ourselves with many layers of identities – our kin, society, ethnicity, culture, language, nation, religion, gender and so on. And we identify ourselves with these at a deep emotional level. Humans have fought many wars to defend these identities. When people fight others to defend their beliefs and identities, that too is idol worship. Saluting a flag with emotion is idol worship. Prayer and worship are not confined to the temple alone. It is a part of life. There are spiritual seekers, who can reach that level of desperation to reach the ultimate Divine experience where they are even ready to die.

There was a man in the state of Bengal, who was maniacally in devotion of Goddess Kali. He reached a threshold of inner experience because he literally did not want to live without the "vision" of the Divine mother. At that point something happened to him. He reached an ecstatic state and the deity became real to him. Later on a master gave him the initiation into the higher dimension where he experienced self-realization. He became known famously as Ramakrishna across India. Now real worship is what Ramakrishna experienced. He was able to enter the gateway into the higher dimension through an extremely intense form of worship. Many deities have appeared real in the inner vision of extremely devout spiritual seekers and some have depicted them in the forms that we see the deities today. Everything in the Hindu religious systems has been a result of someone's inner vision during deep spiritual experience. What they experienced and envisioned have become deities in many places across the land. Not only deities, but also mantras, Yantras, Pranayama techniques, yogic postures etc. are a result of experience in a higher dimension.

24 DEITIES AND HIGHER DIMENSIONS

The first thing that strikes any outsider in the Hindu system is the multitude of Gods and the various attributes that they carry. In addition to the more popular deities like Shiva and Vishnu, there are many more deities that are local. Sometimes mythology would be added to include the local deity into the mainstream Hindu systems. Most people know that these deities were initiated by local spiritual masters who entered the higher dimension through their interaction with or use of such deities. Not only deities, but also animals, rivers, trees, mountains etc. become revered in the same fashion. People followed these masters and watched every move of theirs. If the master visited a place, it became important. If he rested somewhere, it became historical. If he took a dip in a river, it became holy. His burial place became a pilgrimage site. His belongings became revered. Such masters are never considered as dead. They are said to have simply "left their bodies" and can be fully aware at all times and guide those who seek spiritual guidance. Buddha became self realized under a Bodhi tree. That tree is revered today, even though Buddhism does not encourage worship of trees. The tooth of Buddha or his hair is preserved in some monasteries and people flock to those places because of their acquired spiritual significance to many.

Most deities are depicted as carrying weapons. A weapon is meant for protection by destroying anything that can be harmful. It can simply be carried as a threat or warning to anyone who has the intention to harm. One feels secure when a security person carries a weapon. There is a benevolent feeling of being protected when those on the side of the law carry weapons. One feels insecure and worried if a weapon is found at the hands of an outlaw or a sick person. Though a weapon's nature is rooted in violence, seeing a weapon at the hands of a deity gives the feeling of being protected. This protection is not from those who are perceived as "others" or enemies. These enemies are within every person – Greed, temptation, anger, selfishness, ruthlessness, addiction and so on. One has to defeat them and be protected from their influence. The weapons depicted at the hands of the deities are symbolic of the protection one seeks from his internal enemies.

An animal is associated with each deity, usually as a vehicle. When looking at that vehicle, one must realize the spiritual message in it. The Eagle represents to sky. The fish represents the water. The turtle represents the withdrawal of senses. The rodent represents the earth. The bull represents determination. The cow represents wealth and nurturing. The swan represents wisdom. The serpent represents energy that is continuously moving and transforming. The dog represents unshakeable loyalty and unconditional love. The peacock represents inner beauty. Crow represents sharing with others. Ants and bees represent working together harmoniously. The elephant represents having all the power and yet not using it to dominate or intimidate others. A lizard that is comfortable crawling on the ceiling without any fear of falling represents the spirit that can defy gravity. A dove represents peace. A tiger represents single-minded pursuit and not seeing anything else but the elusive target of spiritual enlightenment. India is full of animals that co-exist with all other beings on the streets, around the temples and sometimes resting comfortably inside drainage and sewerage. A spiritual seeker will sense the message in every one of them and remain mindful of his inner pursuit. The environment has a message and it is up to everyone to sense this message. When that message is sensed in everything, spiritual progress becomes continuous.

Every God rides on a vehicle or is seated on something. And each God is associated with certain elements. One would find elements associated with water for Vishnu. He carries a conch shell, which belongs to the ocean. He is shown as lying on a bed of snake in a white colored ocean. Two of his avatars are associated with the ocean (the tortoise and the fish). Shiva is mostly associated with the mountain, especially the Himalayas. He is also associated with the funeral pyre, which is an element of permanent transformation. What goes into the fire is transformed. Brahma is associated with nothing. Saraswati is depicted as seated on a lotus, which represents the state of non-attachment. A lotus can grow in muddy water. But even water cannot wet it. One can be in the world with all its muddy issues. A yogi is unaffected by any of it. A lotus represents that state of wisdom. Ganesh is depicted, as having the head of an elephant with a human body and next to him is a tiny mouse that does not wander around. Amongst land animals today, the elephant is the largest and the mouse is the smallest. The smallest and the largest come together through the human spiritual experience when one sees the image of Ganesh.

Multiple hands depict the capability to handle many things once one reaches the height of spiritual attainment. We ourselves are performing multiple tasks at the same time without noticing them. We are breathing. Our internal organs are performing their actions on their own and working in synchronization with each other. Our mind and consciousness are active. There is no haphazard way of functioning. Each one of us, as an individual system appear many handed, each hand representing an action – respiration, digestion, elimination, protection, transformation, growth and so on. If we can be capable of doing so many things at the same time, the deities symbolize that and beyond. The three heads of the Gods represent being able to sense everything in all realms of time – past, present and the future. They also represent the state of Samadhi in which one's awareness spreads in all directions. Head is the part that carries the awareness. Therefore depicting an expanded awareness is done by multiple heads.

One does not judge a religion based on its followers. Typical Hindus operate at the street level and literally pray to the various deities, not knowing why things are the way they are. Many fail to sense the messages from everything around them, which are like sun's light falling everywhere. Everyone believes in magic and expect miracles to happen. It is all right, considering the state of spiritual development in most people. Some people do question the various beliefs. I have seen people ask, "If God is all mighty and powerful, then why do they lock the temple doors?" Or sometimes when major calamities occur, similar questions would erupt, "If God is there to protect His children, and there are many stories in mythology saying so, where is that God now?" These are valid questions. But if one tried to get answers to street level questions from people with street level spiritual development, it would be like two children arguing about which cartoon character is more valiant.

Most of what is being depicted does not refer to anything at the physical level. However, they have to describe everything with things that are there at the physical level. It is the starting point and not the end in itself. We cannot help using our eyes, or ears or feelings. We cannot help imagining. These are our representational systems. This is what we use to communicate with each other. We know that green means "Go" and red means "Stop." We know that chaos would result if signals were not used. In India, even with signals, chaos prevails on roads. But that is a different topic. Having signals helps in organizing the flow of traffic in somewhat limited way. If people followed the rules, life would be a lot easier. But when everyone is for himself and when survival instinct begins to persist at all times, chaos would be the result.

Religions are like traffic signals. They help people follow a patterned flow that allows everyone to have a fair share of the road and they allow people to choose their different destinations and go in their directions as smoothly as possible. Religions, like traffic signals, do not become the destinations themselves. Many cannot sense this truth. Their arguments with others defending their beliefs are similar to arguing about the pros and cons of green and red signal lights. Traffic happens only on the road or the street level anyway. Inside everyone's home, the rules change. The same filth left on the streets does not enter one's home. It is kept quite clean. A home is something one uses to dwell, rest and stay when not venturing out for survival. People are able to make this distinction between the street and the home. No one has to teach them. All the chaos belongs to the street. Once inside one's home, the first thing one seeks is rest. People want to come home and crash out. Home is a resting place.

If religion can be like the street signals then home is like the inner mind. Between these two, lies the reality of life. If the home carries the same noise and chaos of the road outside, how would one feel at home? Many are carrying their "homes" or inner minds, which is restless and chaotic. Life can be stressful even at home. Everyone seeks peace and harmony. Everyone seeks a spiritual home. Only many cannot find it easily and remain on the chaos of the street. That is why temples become important. One may find more peace in a temple than in his own home. One can be free from chores and day-to-day issues with others in the home. In the temple, chaos is minimal because it is "God's" abode. In some temples silence is insisted. People try not to chat or socialize in such temples. The circumstances change as soon as one leaves home, crosses the streets and enters the temple. If people go to temples often, they manage to find the peace they are looking for. In some, that peace begins to settle within and they are able to go outside, carrying that peace with them. Such people begin to think of others. They help others. They spend more time pondering about the meaning behind it all. And such people can influence others into thinking and feeling the same way.

There is the street or the drama of real life. There is the home or one's inner mind. And there is the higher dimension or the temple. Temples and deities are meant for a reason. They are not mere buildings. The deities are not mere statues. There is a subtle inner process that goes on in every individual as one cycles between the street, his home and the temple. Which one of these begins to occupy his interest depends upon what his spiritual development is. It varies from one person to another. Many remain on the street. Some end up staying at home. Very few end up going to the temple. And amongst those very few, even fewer get to go into the inner sanctum of the temple. There they begin to understand the meaning behind it all. When they do, all they have is love for all. They do not get arrogant about those who prefer to remain at the street level or stay home. They know that everyone does not get to go that far.

Though everyone carries the potential to reach the inner sanctum, they just do not. That is the way the Universe is.

Leaves come and go as seasons change. Flowers bloom and go. Seeds abound and spread in all directions. But the tree remains and grows. We are like seeds. The way the Universe operates is by increasing the chances for something to happen. The more there are, then the more are the chances of something happening with them. Trees and plants emit countless seeds in all directions. Every seed has the necessary ingredients for becoming another tree. But almost all of them simply fall in random places and become wasted. But there are always a few seeds that have the chance to fall in places that have the right conditions for germination. Amongst those that manage to sprout, some will perish young, by being eaten or trampled upon by animals or die from natural causes like illness, lightning, fire or flood. The more the seeds, the more are the chances for another tree to emerge.

In space one finds countless stars. Upon further exploration, one finds even more planets, and even more rocks and dust. From these, stars and planets emerge. And everything does not turn into a star or a planet. Everything that turns into a star varies in size. Everything that turns into a planet is unique like our fingerprints. Somewhere, somehow a planet has the right ingredients and conditions for living organisms to emerge. Multitude increases the possibility of something emerging. We are 6 billion people on this planet. Most lead a mundane life. Very few reach the heights. The potential to reach the heights is there in each one of us. But only a few get to realize their true potential and even amongst them there are fewer who succeed in making it real. Multitude increases the chances for a handful of yogis, visionaries, leaders, Nobel laureates etc. to emerge. These few people in turn shift the flow of the world in the intended direction. They are the ones who trigger the dawn of a higher consciousness.

There are very few people whose creative efforts bear fruit. Even though there is a creative aspect in every individual, very few manage to express it and have an impact on others. So long as creative efforts are pursued with a goal to make this world more beautiful, more aware and more knowledgeable, everything works wonderfully. But then creative people and their works are a minority. The majority simply enjoys the fruits of creative efforts and do not contribute much. Many are engaged in sustaining what has been created while very few amongst them create something more out of it.

One can change the natural process slightly and increase the chance of more seeds sprouting and becoming mature trees. All one has to do is to create a farm and rely on the bees and insects to do the job of pollination and harvest the products. Deities, mantras, Yantras, rituals, festivals, mythology, scriptures etc. are the various fertilizers and nutrients used to run this farm for spiritual development. That is the purpose of religions – to enhance the chance for spiritual growth. But these farms cannot have fences. Fences cause limitations. Religions are rooted on spirituality, which is unlimited. This fenceless freedom causes weeds to grow in them and take away the nutrients. Every deity is energized with cosmic energy using ritualistic procedures and that energy is sustained by certain more procedures and the devotional spirit of the people who flock to those temples. The spiritual energy incorporated into a deity can have healing powers and can trigger spiritual advancement in some who are ready for it. There are temples in India where people have been going for generations spanning over a thousand or more years. There is always someone in the crowd who is gaining spiritual advancement. As time goes, corruption sets in and it begins to drain the cosmic energy away from the temple. Sometimes it can go to the extent of being desecrated and demolished. There are many temples strewn across India that have been left as ruins. Corruption can lead to destruction and ruin.

Nature works through the process of nucleation and growth. Everything carries the potential for nucleation. But it occurs only in some depending upon where the favorable circumstances and the potential to sprout merge. Across the countless multitude, somewhere here and there, new awareness nucleates in some and then it spreads around. Growth happens depending upon favorable conditions again. If there are enough people with the potential to receive, then growth becomes rapid. At some stage growth has spread in every direction and the new awareness becomes the norm and the previous stages of awareness become sporadic. Then more nucleation happens with even higher potential for awareness if the conditions are fertile and favorable. Disruptions stem such progress. They too are part of nature. Disruptions allow for readjustment and change in direction according to times.

One can see this in everything in the Universe. Among the countless galaxies, stars and planets, the dice rolled correctly and the earth won the jackpot. Life thrives on this planet. As we look around, nothing else seems to have the same potential conditions for organic life. They all indicate how precarious our existence is and how fortunate we are and how wonderful it feels to be aware of it. No other animal on this planet seems to be aware of this precious gift of life we all have been blessed with. And how fortunate we are to carry that potential to realize the Universe within us and connect with that consciousness!

We are all seeds carrying the same potential for greater awareness. But only in some of us the potential finds the favorable conditions and a new dimension of consciousness sprouts. The others get strewn in all directions. The tree of life keeps spreading the seeds of higher awareness in all directions, carried by the wind of life current and some of them do fall at the right place and become trees of wisdom themselves. We are all like the millions of sperm swimming against the odd and one manages to reach that egg of wisdom and a new embryo of consciousness happens. Everything seems random. Yet in this randomness, there is the tendency for order and structure. Symmetric balance arises when forces neutralize each other. One can choose to exist without caring for any of this and the Universe does not punish him for it. It has given him the freedom to choose. He too carries the seed of higher wisdom. But there are plenty more carrying the same.

25 GATEWAYS TO HIGHER DIMENSIONS

God is just a reference point for us to help advance our awareness. As to how God must look, there is no fixed rule in Hindu systems. God or deity can be in any form as per the mindset of each individual. It can be a yogi. It can be three headed. It can be a dancer. It can be a loving mother. It can be a baby. It can be a warrior. It can be a romantic hero. It can be a guru. It can be a terrifying woman, drinking blood and having a garland made up of chopped heads. It can be anthropomorphic. It can be a number. It can be a syllable. It can be a geometric pattern. It can just be a place or a river. It can be a ritual. It can be fire. It can be formless. All these are reference coordinates for different spiritual seekers to start their journey from whichever state of mind they are at.

Some of these images and symbols correspond to different emotions. And emotions can be gateways into the higher realms of spirituality. Emotion is needed to breathe life into anything. When one reads a text, if it is read without expressing the emotions involved, it sounds bland and lifeless. Emotions carry expressions, which are the essence of the living experience. When thoughts and emotions merge, it is felt both in the body and the mind. Feeling is an experience of an emotion or thought. Every thought carries an emotion with it.

The Bhakti movement in India relies on the emotion of pure devotion. A devotee following such a path can frame himself into a loving mother or a passionate romantic who cannot fall in love with anyone other than the Divine. Prayer songs that are sung with drum beats and cymbals can be therapeutic. The conscious mind slowly lets go as one engages in group singing and reaches a stage where the surroundings are forgotten and devotion begins to overwhelm the mind and spirit. It is a gateway into the higher realm. One can only show devotion towards something as a subject. One cannot fall in love with a stone. But one can surely feel that emotion towards another being. Whether that being is there or not is not the purpose. If one began to feel such an emotion of love inside and began to experience it by interacting with a higher being, then ordinary love turns into devotion. By actively immersing oneself into singing and dancing, a devotee can feel the higher dimension. Bhakti movement does not rely on rituals and physical exercise, discipline etc. One just gets into singing and praying to reach an ecstatic state. It appeals to some people and they follow that path where no one is judged or discriminated. The deity for devotion can be in the form of a romantic lover. Or the deity can take the form of a loving mother.

There are those who try to transcend the emotion of fear as their path to the same thing. They adorn themselves with frightening imagery and pray during hours when everyone is afraid to venture out. Their God images appear gory and violent. Some conduct their rituals in cremation grounds. They attempt to experience fear to the fullest and go past it. When they do, they realize there is no such thing as fear and it is the same Divinity that is experienced by other paths.

There are those who inflict pain on themselves to transcend into the next dimension. Some practice consuming poison in a controlled way and try to transcend to the higher level. There are methods in Tantra where the practitioners ingest Arsenic, Mercury etc. slowly to gain control over their effects. There are those who try to transcend using sexual orgasm. Some discard all these and simply pursue meditation. Some take to yoga and Pranayama. Some take to selfless service to others. There are any pathways to choose from. No one can compare them and analyze them as better or worse. Analysis causes one to become distant from direct experience.

Everyone will find a path that suits his or her inner constitution. That path will open for them when spiritual currents get triggered in them at their own appropriate time through their life cycles, experience, karma and exposure from the surroundings.

In Hindu religions, whoever set up the various deities, scriptures, rituals, prayers, places of worship, practices etc. have cleverly hidden the ultimate purpose, which is to discern the connectivity between us and the Universe around us. We are like ocean water confined to a sealed bottle floating on the ocean itself. If we crack the bottle to reconnect, we call it death. The different spiritual practices have evolved to enable that connectedness be experienced without cracking the bottle open, while being alive. What seems separate is connected to everything around. This layer of separation can be transcended by spiritual pursuit. And this pursuit begins in everyone at some point, based on his or her own individuality, inclinations and surroundings. If the surroundings have ample ingredients to stimulate those inclinations to pursue transcendence, then it enhances the chances for many such individuals to go beyond mundane existence. The Hindu religions have such ingredients set up in all walks of life.

Everything does not have to be explained. The rational mind, driven by the ego wants an explanation or a definition of everything. Explanation lessens the effect of experiencing. Understanding through explanation or description is limited. Understanding by experiencing is limitless. And if that experience happens on its own it has a more profound effect on an individual. A sensation can be explained on a relative scale of one to ten. But it can be experienced to the fullest. The rational mind tries to understand everything in a relativistic dimension. It simply cannot understand much when its coordinates are taken out. A child experiences more and learns rapidly as a result.

The methodology in Hindu religious systems is to keep things as simple as possible at the initial stages so that learning becomes an internal process. One experiences what is being taught indirectly by using what is available around and that experience relates to average day-to-day experience. Imagine teaching a four year old the idea of numbers, addition and subtraction. The child is blank in this regard. It has no idea what we are trying to teach. It can only learn from what it can relate to and experience at its level of awareness. A lot of us brush aside complexity by calling it as Rocket science.

The different gateways are like vehicles. One can reach a building nearby by going in one direction. He can also reach it by going around the world. A vehicle helps get to a destination faster. It represents the process of transcending something. One can go over the surface of the ocean on a boat, being rocked and tossed around by the wind and the waves. One can also take a submarine and have a smooth ride. Likewise, one can travel by ground in a bus or a car or a train. Or he could take a flight. Each vehicle has its advantages in terms of speed, comfort and cost. Likewise spiritual progress has many such vehicles using which one can accelerate the process of transcendence. One's own body is one such vehicle. Our minds are another. Every emotion is a vehicle as well. These vehicles help us reach intermediate transit points. The destination is still ahead.

The emphasis in Hindu religions is not to explain everything. One can however, describe something on his or her own terms. Describing an experience is easier than explaining it. Western systems set out to find an explanation for everything observed. Eastern systems were content with simply describing the experience of observation. Intuition and wisdom can be quickly enhanced through internal experience and if needed a description in the simplest way is adequate. That description may not explain the same thing to someone else. But anyone who has had a similar internal experience will find that description resonating within. That is how understanding happens. No one sets out verifying what has been described. One among the many will find the description causing an internal resonance. The Eastern systems found that to be adequate.

Being in a spiritual mindset continuously, being conscious of it all the time is an essential step for an aspiring seeker. It can be accomplished easily if one set up an environment around himself that constantly reminds his inner mind about spiritual elements - bells, sounds, colors, value systems, daily activities, what is being consumed, who he interacts with and so on. In the Hindu system, they have set up the Divine names in the form of syllables that serve one such purpose. Some of these syllables are linked to certain

Nadis and chakras. Names of places, rivers, mountains and even animals are chosen this way. Some Nadis in the ethereal human body have same name as some holy rivers that run in the Indian subcontinent.

There have been times when the whole land has been treated as a human body. The entire sub-continent has been related to a human body, not just the physical one, but the astral aspects included. The mountain in the North became the head. The rivers became the Nadis. Places like Nepal are still undergoing that kind of experiment. Some have taken the whole cosmos as the body. Here the celestial bodies, their conjunction, transit etc. become important. Stars, eclipses etc. are considered as important links to what happens at the individual level. One's whole body becomes a temple. A temple is constructed like a body. Then the whole land is treated as one. And finally the whole cosmos becomes a body as well. All put together is one body we call as Shiva. This body is physical as well as unmanifest (symbolized as Ardha-Nari-Ishwara, half male and half female). By starting at the individual body level, one is able to reach into the Universe in steps.

26 INTELLIGENCE

Multitude, proliferation, potential, favorable conditions, nucleation and growth are the way the Universe operates. Intelligence or wisdom operates at an extremely fundamental level. Universal intelligence is not complex. It is extremely simple, like the microprocessors in computers functioning at the fundamental level of one and zero. Yet the computer can execute tasks at incredible speeds just using those ones and zeros. So does the universe using the fundamental intelligence based on manifest and unmanifest consciousness. The Hindus call this by various names - Shakti and Shiva, Lakshmi and Vishnu and Saraswati and Brahma.

There are seven notes in music. But from those seven notes, an infinite variety of music can be generated. And that music can evoke a variety of emotions just by listening. We can train a monkey to play the seven notes back and forth. But the monkey will not go beyond that. It cannot improvise. Imagine this. If we only played those seven notes in a sequence back and forth during a concert, do you think you will pay for it? We humans are like those seven notes. Out of us, an infinite variety of potential can be extracted. If we choose to play at the basic seven-note level, realize how much is being wasted away. Our inner spirit does not allow that to happen. It pushes us from within to do something. Each one of us is like an individual song composed out of those seven notes. Each one of us is unique because those seven notes can be combined in infinite permutations. Some of us have lost proper tuning and turned into cacophony. Some have become number one hits on the charts. Our tendencies are driven by how well tuned we are and how good a song we become through the manipulation of those seven notes in us. Intelligence is a fundamental structure out of which an infinite combination of orderly variations can be created. The Universe might look chaotic and random in every direction. But order happens through the process of intelligence. Atoms form. Stars go through a sequence to create heavier atoms. Objects orbit to achieve gravitational balance. Crystals form. Rainbow shows an orderly change in color. Body cells form ordered shapes and not random ones. Everything is like music and dance. The reason why we humans like music and dance is because we can relate to the fundamental intelligence of the Universe through them. That is how the Universe operates. Music and dance give us a glimpse of that fundamental nature of the Universe. We are ordered structures and we understand why.

A piano has sets of keys, each set corresponding to different octaves. Each set has seven notes. If one just played the seven notes in a sequence, it would sound pleasing, but one wouldn't call it music. If one played the notes in a haphazard manner, one wouldn't call it music either. Real music arises when one plays the notes by selecting them to express moods, emotions, tempo and pace. All that music now arises not in the piano, but in the consciousness of the player who is moving her fingers deftly on the keys without even looking at them. She has breathed life into the piano and its keys. Without the player, the piano is just a dead instrument. Her rendition of the music arose from her inner realm and expressed through the playing of the keys makes music. It is an inner experience that is revealing itself through the player and the keys. Our own existence is similar. We are like the piano and its seven keys. Unless life force plays through us, we simply will not be active.

All that is amazingly complex and looks like an artwork does not need to be designed and crafted by some super intelligent being. Something can evolve into that ultimate complex mechanism through the process of evolution by basing itself on very fundamental state of intelligence. If a religion that has so many indirect reasons for the way things are set up, it does not mean a

Prophet of incredible power sat and created everything in it. Our human bodies are a product of slow evolution. No one can doubt that today.

Creation means there is a starting point somewhere. It is a simplistic street view, which is all right at the first grade level of spirituality. It is a view from a dualistic reference frame where there is a point of origin and the coordinates relative to it. Creation is a continuous process and it happens in very small and simple increments. Everything is being created, while overlapping with everything that has been created and interacting with each other. There is no linear sequence. We human beings create things – works of art, inventions, writings and so on. We design, plan and execute. We have a timeline to complete. Therefore we tend to perceive the Universe from the same human vantage point of having a grand Creator who took a deep breath and breathed life into everything. And according to this human perspective, He is said to have created everything in a certain number of days.

When one says the word "Creation" it seems like an event in the past. Every instant is creation. It is a continuous process. Things are being created all the time. Every thought is a creation. When something is continuous it cannot be looked at as having an origin. For those who believe in an origin, they must try the exercise of finding a starting point on the perimeter of a circle. When they find that starting point, they will know when creation happened. Creation and Dissolution are happening together. Creation, existence and dissolution are the aspects of the manifest. Something manifests, it exists and then it dissolves away. As it is doing, another thing manifests and goes through the same cycle. Beings are not born at the same time, living through the same extent of time and dying at the same time so that the next batch starts. It is an ongoing process. Generations overlap. A child born in a large family might be in the same generation as the grandparent for another child born to someone older in the same family.

The analytical approach to understand the Universe is to compartmentalize everything and characterize it. We like to see a circle in segments rather than as a continuum. It makes measurement easy. This does not mean that is how nature works. Nature is made up of overlaps and interconnectedness. Everything penetrates into everything else. All vehicles go on the same road at different speeds. It looks chaotic. But that is how nature also works. Order and chaos go on at the same time in the same place. The two extremes go together in nature everywhere. Randomness sets up the imbalance and order restores the balance. Going from balance to imbalance and back to balance is nothing but steps in a dance. When one looks at the statue of Shiva in a dancing posture, it represents that cosmic dance.

If one were to observe a personal computer, it does amazing things. It is used for many purposes. All the one does with a computer in general is to make an input and get a response. A keyboard and a mouse are the general input means. Most of us do not care about what the computer does. We use it as a tool to get some work done for us. There are some who think the monitor is the computer because all the output is displayed on the monitor. The computer is a box inside which there are circuit boards and electronic chips, along with memory storage. There is software that links the input and makes the circuits and chips in the computer to provide the desired output on the screen. If one were to dig deeper into how everything works, he will go past the simplicity of input and output and see the layers of software that have been developed to accomplish the desired results. Beyond the software lies the core-processing unit called microprocessor. If one were to dig into the microprocessor, it will become evident that it is a chip that has millions of electronic circuits and devices packaged into a tiny space.

If one went further, the entire principle of everything is based on just two numbers – 1 and 0. It is called as Digital Electronics where logic circuits are created to function between two states of electricity – under a potential and no potential. Potential is measured in volts. 1 corresponds to a certain value, which can be as low as a thousandth of a volt. 0 means the circuit is off. It is like flipping a light switch off and on. The speed at which this flipping happens is incredible. It can be several million such operations in one second. It is not obvious to someone looking at the computer monitor to realize that all of it is made up of 1s and 0s at a high frequency. Intelligence operates at a similar fundamental level – manifest and unmanifest. Everything is derived off of this fundamental state at which the Universe operates.

We are like the result displayed on the screen. We also become our own input mechanisms. We process the information using a software code called life. Just like every computer needs a power supply connected to an electrical outlet, which in turn is connected to a power grid, we are all connected to the Universe from which we derive our source of life to function.

The largest objects in the sky are made up of the tiniest of atoms. Every star is made up of Hydrogen atoms. And every Hydrogen atom, if looked into further is made up of energy packets that appear and disappear between the states of manifest and unmanifest. The largest and the smallest are together in stars in the sky. The energy contained in the tiniest atomic nucleus can wipe out an entire city. One does not know why it all has to be that way. All one can do is observe and record. The unknown seems to be like the rainbow one is trying to touch.

The yogi is not interested in knowing what the elements in the Periodic Table are or how they came into existence. He has no interest in figuring out when the first atom appeared and out of what. To a yogi, the goal is to realize the Universal connectivity within. The shape and characteristics of the Universe do not matter. It can be anything. He is like the fish in the ocean. The fish has its own consciousness and awareness. It feels separate. Yet it is part of that ocean. By expanding the awareness, the yogi understands the wholeness of everything. Beyond that there is nothing to explore. All that matters is the inner experience that takes him to the source of the fundamental intelligence. It is something that can only be realized by inner experience. Words are extremely limited to describe it. And one definitely cannot explain it. A droplet is good enough to know all about the ocean.

In some schools of thought in India, they use an inward questioning method that asks, "Who is doing the thinking?" One reaches a point where he cannot point at anything. Even the word "who" tends to symbolize an entity. Words cannot describe beyond a point. That which cannot be quantified cannot be addressed even by the word, "who". But that inward questioning leads one towards an inner experience that can trigger the knowing. There are many words to describe that state – "Nothingness", "Stillness", "Nirvana", "Shunya", "Satori", "Enlightenment", "Buddha" and so on.

When Buddha was asked about God, he simply maintained silence. Because the answer was contained in that silence. "God" is a word and it only points to something. There is something even beyond words and unfortunately we have to call it by a word. It is known as awareness. People refer to this awareness as all knowing. As soon as one says, "All knowing," questions arise. How about solving some difficult math equations? How about revealing all the winning numbers for the jackpot? How about predicting who wins the championship? That is not the awareness or all-knowing capability. That is a limited definition in the mind of a limited human being.

The all-knowing awareness operates at the most fundamental level. It is simply the realization of the connectivity between the individual and everything that surrounds it. A realized person cannot speak in every language in the world. Nor can he say for sure what is at the edge of the visible universe. Even if he did, no one can verify that. One either believes what he says or he does not. Every realized yogi is still in the body. When in the body, its limitations still remain.

It is only when a yogi reaches into his inner realm, can he connect with the Universe and become one with it at will. He can reach the ultimate depth of calmness or beyond and simply experience it fully. And he needs nothing from this material world after that. He does not worry about his body dying. He knows it will die one day. But his awareness can transcend that mortal end. He can now live forever in full awareness even after the body has been discarded. A yogi lives his life to the fullest extent while in his body. As a result, even the mortal death simply becomes an experience that he can go through with full awareness. When it is over, that awareness still remains. He realizes that there is no need for him to be born again in a limited body when he has realized the unlimited. We call this state as immortality. It is not something one can do by being in the body forever. It is the ability to remain aware and alive without the need for a body forever.

27 AWARENESS

The word "God" itself has been abused so much that it brings derision in some people. Instead, let us call it the Universe. We all know we are a part of the Universe. We know it exists. As to its dimensions, we are too small to gauge it. Our only interest must be to feel connectivity to the Universe. Like fish swimming inside water, we exist in the Universe depending entirely on the resources that it provides. There is not one thing that we do not take from this Universe to be really independent in any way. As soon as one thinks of the Universe, the image of Godhead simply disappears. This Universe is all consciousness out of which we have a limited awareness of a band within its spectrum.

Hindu temples resemble the whole path to reach the summit of awareness. They are surrounded by the streets where everyone generally starts. Then there are entrances through which those who want to avoid the chaos of the streets enter. They go through the long corridors around the temple. Temples have towers that are trapezoidal in shape, wide at the bottom and pointed towards the top, much like a mountain that has many paths at its base. The inner sanctum symbolizes the spiritual core in every human. The corridors, deities, bells, drums, colors, smells etc. symbolize the Nadis and Chakras in the body that lead one to the inner sanctum. Many go into the temple, pray and go about their lives. One who becomes aware of the purpose of it all, finds his / her whole body to be a temple. He then does not need to go to the temple and offer his prayers there anymore. He/she becomes a seeker.

A believer transitions into a seeker through the continued exposure to the spiritual realm from the environment. A seeker does not believe. His goal is not to believe but to know. Knowing happens by direct internal experience. Belief happens when we are told by others. However, belief is the stepping-stone towards becoming a seeker. Belief system is like graduating through different grades from pre-school all the way to a graduate degree. Then one gets ready to do a PhD. This is the state of the seeker. One spends considerable time preparing to become a PhD candidate. It takes almost two decades to get to that level for an average person. In spiritual realm, life experience is the school and the teacher. Religions, scriptures, mythology, philosophy etc. are the textbooks to learn from. Not everyone sees the need to get a PhD. And even amongst spiritual PhDs, very few become Nobel Laureates. That is the way everything is. Base is where one is grounded. To escape from the gravity of mortal life is extremely difficult. One has to take the efforts to climb the mountain of spiritual journey and reach the summit. There is gravity there at the summit too. But one can fly from it with a glider if he chooses to, defying that gravitational pull of sense based existence.

Awareness expands in an individual who realizes the link between the limited self and the Universe in which he exists temporarily. The real essence of the Hindu systems is the effort to become aware in an unlimited fashion. There are more believers than seekers. But believers can become seekers. If everyone set about seeking, the real world cannot function. Everything happens through the drama of life. Through the living process that involves interactions with others, choices made, actions taken, effects experienced, the learning from such experiences and further stages of drama, one ascends the mountain of wisdom. Once the timberline is crossed, the believer transitions into a seeker. One has to be like a warrior beyond this stage, knowing well that higher elevation causes the most dramatic fall, being focused, with discipline, seeking guidance and finally reaching the summit. One gets to see everything from the summit, the way an eagle sees, but with the wisdom and consciousness of a human.

It is always important to start from one's natural state using his natural inclinations. Why do we like happiness? It is our natural state. Why do we like love, life, compassion, empathy, courage etc.? They belong to the natural state of the human consciousness plane. If a lion kills a prey, it does so only when it is hungry. Otherwise it sits quiet even if all the prey is wandering nearby. To kill to feed itself is its natural state. A lion does not kill otherwise. Everything exists in its natural state. When something is done or a choice of action is made within the bounds of one's natural state, it is called Dharma. When we deviate from it, we enter the field of karma. Karma means, to do. When a soldier kills during a war to protect himself and his people, it becomes a natural action under the law of Dharma. If one kills for pleasure, it is a deliberate choice, outside the bounds of Dharma. If we did anything the natural way, we are at peace. As soon as we deviate from it, suffering results. Suffering is a reminder to return to the natural state. Even enjoyment is a form if suffering. If one lied down all the time, that is wonderful. But we would feel groggy after sometime. Our natural state is that of righteous action and balance. The natural state of everything in the Universe is to be in balance where the net force is nil and energy tends towards its lowest level.

Why does one have to struggle and conquer? It brings experience and learning. A windy road going up and down makes one drive with alertness and gain more experience driving his vehicle. A smooth, straight road leads to comfort, boredom and yawn. If one went to a movie where all that was shown on the screen was the hero sleeping on the bed, would that make it an interesting story? Why do we seek drama, story and adventure? A quest is always in our spirit. It is the spirit that is seeking answers in order to gain experience. Any new experience brings the child in us. To a child everything is new, including the most trivial thing from our view. New experience was hitherto unknown. Any exposure to something new arouses curiosity and the desire to experience and know more. The quest for the unknown is rooted in the spirit. Awareness increases through each and every experience.

The purpose of Karma is not to hold us back. It is meant to

trigger awareness in us. This is much like pain. Pain is there to prevent us from over exerting a part that is hurt and is in the process of healing. If one did not feel the pain, they will completely damage that part. Karma limits us from deviating from our spiritual dimension. But it does so without directing anyone. Awareness has to happen within each individual through experience.

Every individual has the fundamental right to seek spiritual progress on his/her own terms and when he or she feels like it. If one chooses not to pursue any of it, the Universe gives them all that freedom. If they choose to be ignorant, it is their privilege. However, freedom invariably gets abused if one chooses to be ignorant. The wise ones understand Dhrama better. If wrongful choice is made due to ignorance, Karma begins to emerge and like body pain, it limits the individual from free movement. This happens until the individual realizes that he or she has created this whole entrapment around himself or herself and the only way to be free is to become aware and not abuse their rights and those of others. The one, who knows how the hot grill feels, is very careful not to repeat that error again. This is self-teaching. Every experience in life is a teacher. One learns internally at his or her own pace. There is no hurry. If one thinks about languages, that is how we learn to speak in a language. No one starts teaching grammar and syntax from the age of one. One learns all that only when they are ready at a higher-grade level. Before that, learning a language happens by indirect experience during childhood. One not only learns words, but also the structure of sentences, adding tonal variations, emotions etc. into expressions. A lot of learning happens through internal experience. And such an experience and learning is imperceptible and permanent in one's mind. They do not think about it. It just happens.

Spiritual development done the same way through one's life experience and continuous exposure to spiritual elements in the environment will always enhance the chances of one leaping forward. Countries that have the culture of sports always generate the best athletes and they bag the maximum medals in any competition. Thus, spiritual development is tied strongly to the culture, religion and social infrastructure. A system like that appears chaotic and lacking in any structure that is not visible from the outside. These factors cannot be independent of each other. One cannot tell where culture ends and religion begins. Everything has to become a part of daily life in order to facilitate the inner change. This is how the natural way works - things are exposed to everyone in every way possible and one learns to associate himself with what is around subliminally. Learning happens imperceptibly, the same way we all learned our mother tongues and some of us became extremely proficient with them.

28 THE INTERMEDIATE STAGE

Seen from a purely street view, the physical body is real and ordinary people cannot sense anything beyond the physical body. Yogis are not considered as part of the norm. Therefore most people dwelling at the street level of awareness leave such aspects to the yogis. There are people who will only accept what they can sense physically. They will negate everything else. In India there is a school of philosophy known as Ca'rvaka where its adherents do precisely that. The Indian system allows for many ideas and philosophies to exist. A few centuries ago, debates would be held between the adherents of different philosophical schools. These debates were popular and many would come to watch them. Those who participated in those debates were highly educated scholars who had spent a vast time of their lives in learning the different philosophical ideas and choosing one of them as making the most sense to them.

Indian philosophical schools can be classified into two main categories – Astika (Based on the primacy of Vedas) and Nastika (Negating the primacy of the Vedas). The Astika (Orthodox) schools include logic based Nyaya, atomistic view based Vaiseshika, dualism based Samkhya, Dharma based Mimamsa, the school of Yoga that involves body, mind and spirit and Vedanta school which deals with the meaning of Vedas and other scriptures based on them. All these schools accept the authority of the Vedas.

The Nastika (Non-Orthodox) schools negate the authority of Vedas. The school of Ca'rvaka is purely materialistic and does not accept the existence of something called God. There are two other Nastika philosophies, which form the basis for the religions of Jainism and Buddhism. Both are atheistic. Unlike Carvaka, Jainism and Buddhism do acknowledge the yogic way of spiritual pursuit. They basically avoid the streets as the starting point. One goes directly into meditative approach for which the knowledge of the spiritual body is needed. The yogis of India follow different orders that are based on Shiva or Vishnu or Shakti. The Jainists and Buddhists follow the monastic tradition. Advanced monks in these two religions do spend their times in caves under meditation. Both philosophies also share the belief in reincarnation and liberation from cycles of birth and death. Jainism follows the principles of non-violence and equality between all life forms.

This entire book can be filled with the various aspects of the Indian philosophical systems. However, it is not the purpose of this writing. I am making only a passing mention about them here. I therefore refer the reader to the many books on Indian philosophy. There are books exclusively on each system of philosophy. One can spend a lifetime just studying one. Philosophy is the intermediate stage where someone begins to ponder about the meaning of life and existence. He has already stepped off from the street. He now has questions. He does not realize at this stage that the answers to most questions can be from within. He seeks the guidance of what is already out there that has been thought of by others before him. Based on one's inclination, any one type of philosophy might be appealing to him. He might find a lot of connectedness to one type of philosophy. Then that view might change based on the argumentative skills of someone well learned from another school of philosophy. At this intermediate stage one interprets everything rather than seek a direct answer from within. It is a stage one goes through. The person on the street definitely has tremendous respect for anyone who has entered the world of philosophy.

In Sanskrit, the word that comes close to meaning philosophy is "Darsana" (vision). The Western philosophy is driven mostly by intellectual analysis of the world around and outward experience. The Indian systems rely on intuitive knowledge based on inward experience. The Western analysis is objective whereas the Indian analysis is subjective and experience based. Western philosophy has driven their world in material progress. It is the philosophical base that has laid the foundation of Western scientific approach. In some ways Western philosophy resembles the Carvaka system in India. Evidence has to be obtained either directly or through deductive logic. Mathematics has been used in the Western system to prove scientific theories, even if material proof cannot be obtained. Mathematics is a result in the Indian philosophical thought and not a tool. Numbers, Geometric patterns etc. are related to spiritual realms in the Indian context. India thus derived the concept of zero through a philosophical view.

It must be mentioned here that there is no such thing as a superior or inferior system. No one sits and decides which way societies must go. Everything happens according to the environment around. In the European cultures, logic and more left brained pursuit of knowledge gained ascendency. In India, more intuition based approach evolved. No one controls evolution. One looked outward for answers and the other one turned inward. As to why each one pursued opposite directions is for someone to ponder about and waste his lifetime over it. What is important to realize is that over the course of time, the two approaches have come to meet and an integration is happening on its own accord. Through the process of integration, things will get even better. The evolution of the Western European society has been strongly influenced by the Greco-Roman system of structure and order.

For the past two thousand years, Roman Empire has had the strongest influence on the cultures in Europe where unity, standardization, structured approach has been a way to conquer and control everyone. Emperor Constantine realized the benefits of such unified approach and adopted Christianity to champion that effort. Organized religion happened in Rome. Just like the imposition of Communism in the USSR, force was used wherever possible to bring societies under control and unity was held together by the fear of others who were outside the boundaries of organized religion. Under rigid enforcement, the underlying cultures took new shape, integrating whatever was imposed. Through this integration, renaissance happened. Here structure, linear approach, referential vision, outward look etc. became the basis for understanding the world around. In that process, industrial revolution, modern science and technology emerged. They in turn helped strengthen the Western philosophical system. When the powers from Europe colonized the rest of the world, native cultures, religious practices and their philosophical systems appeared exotic and strange. However, through the process of interaction over centuries, a better understanding and learning has emerged. Going forward, the world will only benefit from the integration of these diametrically opposite approaches towards spiritual experience. Anytime extremes come together, they always provide an opening for a new awakening to dawn.

Intellectual analysis is discouraged in the Hindu system. Intellectualism leads to more questions than answers. It prevents intuition to take root. Intuition or Buddhi (Wisdom) is rooted in spirit. Education in ancient India was based on intuitive methods. Even now, traditional arts, medicine, music, dance etc. are taught using age-old methods based on intuitive development. India's ancient scriptures were verbally taught for a long time. Disciple-Guru system of learning was the norm. Disciples lived with their teachers, serving them and learning was not confined to any fixed hours. It was continuous. Martial arts, Spiritual training, vocational crafts were also taught the same way. This led to extraordinary skills and capabilities. Sharp memory was an aspect of it. People in the past generations had excellent memory. Most of what they learned was taught initially by rote and repetition. Then intuition was allowed to settle in. This led to the generation of great artists and performers. The whole science of Ayurveda, the Indian traditional medical system, was taught the same way over generations. Going past the stages of interest and learning real spiritual practices through Pranayama, Yoga etc. are taught even now the same way.

Ancient Indians built massive temples, full of incredible sculpture. All were built using intuitive methods where the design, plan, choice of material and construction were based on no writing, drawing or recording. Temples were built according to a system known as Agama Shastra. One learned the rules of the system by being disciples and registering everything taught in the mind. Writing down notes was not the norm and was discouraged. Indian classical music was taught the same way. One spent many years with a master, learning every intricate aspect of the music, performed with the master and one day was blessed by the master to go out and perform independently. Such disciples themselves became great masters on their own accord. Pundit Ravi Shankar, who is famous across the world for Sitar, is a product of such a system.

There is always a spiritual aspect attached to everything in that system whether it is day-to-day functioning or skills or arts. Traditional music, dance and performances are an essential part of festivals in India. They were based on the mythological stories that are known all across the land. Everything has been set up towards an intuition-based approach. One learns by direct experience. There are famous people known for their contribution in many fields. However, there are many more who contributed to the development of these areas without taking any credit. In most Indian temples, one will never know the names of the architects and sculpture. The only names associated with them would be those of kings and emperors who sponsored their construction. It must be remembered that a genius relies entirely on intuition. Every prodigy can do amazing things, but has no idea how he does it. He is somehow able to reach deep into his intuitive realm and everything simply appears to him. This is universal. In every society there have been such people who came up with incredible things.

Modern India has taken up the Western method of teaching which is structured to offer equal opportunities to everyone and employs teachers with varying skills and knowledge. Intuition based teaching is minimal. India under British colonization has undergone changes in many ways. Traditional ways in India have found recognition in the Western world due to this interaction. What was confined to the shores of India is attracting seekers from across the world. There are Indian yogis who have gone to the West and trained people in the traditions of yoga and meditation. Many Westerners have sought spiritual guidance and have flocked to India. With the advent of technology, there is a lot more access to the traditional methods of India, which are slowly beginning to gain recognition and respect across the world. The science of spiritual quest has happened in many parts of the world. However, in India it has reached an advanced level and has been maintained by a system of saints and yogis over eons.

What was once looked at with derision and contempt is now getting recognition and respect across the world. This is a great step forward. The whole world is headed in the direction of better awareness and interconnectedness. People are able to choose a path according to their inclinations and leanings. There are many Westerners who have become full-fledged yogis in their own right. There is tremendous sincerity and dedication to reach the pinnacle of human spiritual experience in many. Technology is facilitating this integration. It is important to be conscious of the benefits to be derived from this integration rather than boast about the superiority of one system over the other. Everything has happened in human consciousness. Therefore it is for humans to benefit tremendously by knowing more about what the world has to offer and enhance their spiritual experiences. Open mindedness is dawning across the world. Many are willing to educate themselves about what the world cultures have to offer and integrate those beneficial aspects into their own day-to-day activities.

At the street level people are going to be pushing and shoving each other. It is the nature of the street. However, as one takes the step into the temple, it is important to let go off the footwear of bias, stay grounded and approach the inner realm with open mind. One also has to let go off expectations. If one approached spiritual realm with expectations of seeing something or experiencing something, they will be back on the street. That is how things on the street are. The unknown has to be approached as it is. It will appear to each individual in its own way based on his or her inner constitution. Being open minded is the first basic need for spiritual journey.

29 THE UNIVERSE WITHIN

A reader, who has come this far, all the way from the street and closer to the inner sanctum, can now understand about the spiritual body. All along I have mentioned certain aspects of it and have not clearly laid out the needed details. This information is available in countless books already. However, in order to go further, this turn is important. I have mentioned so far about going from the physical dimension to the meta-physical and spiritual dimensions. I started from the street where the reality describes the way the world is – a lot more in belief and very little desire to seek. At that level, it is all right not to know everything. Continued exposure and indirect learning happens extremely slowly. There is no hurry. Once life's experience begins to push some people into becoming curious about what is behind that experience, they begin to seek answers inwardly. That is like taking the steps inside the temple or deciding to climb the mountain.

Even at this stage, many go back and forth between the street and the entrance. Some enter deeper. Things begin to make some sense. They are still hesitant. The desire to be go back to the street is still strong. This is the stage of the philosopher. Then comes a stage where one gets venturesome and crosses the main entrance once in for all. After this, life opens up more. Guidance begins to happen. With guidance, the believer slowly transitions into a seeker. Then the eagerness to seek accelerates. At some point, they decide to go all

the way in. This transition is facilitated by the connectivity with the Universe.

The Universe is connected to us through our spiritual layers, which are collectively called as the Astral or Ethereal body. The physical body is known as Bhuta Sharira in Sanskrit. There are five layers surrounding the physical body. If one wonders where it all became known, I can only refer to the yogis who have mentioned about them in different works for the benefit of others. In Sanskrit they are known as "Kosha". The first one is our physical body that is sustained by food (Annamaya Kosha). The layer surrounding the body is sustained by the life force or Prana (Pranamaya Kosha). Prana travels through the 72000 Nadis in the Pranic layer. Prana enters and exits in relation to our breathing. The sheath surrounding this layer is related to one's sub-conscious mind. It is linked to our sensory organs from which information is continuously being registered in this layer (known as Manomaya Kosha).

Generally people associate mind with the brain. However, the Hindu systems consider the brain just as an organ that acts as a channel for the spiritual layers. Some memory is associated with the brain. However, most memory belongs to the Manomaya Kosha. This memory includes everything from this life as well as all memories from the previous incarnations. It is possible to tap into these past life memories through deep meditation. Awareness begins to expand and reaches the outer layers. By deeply relaxing oneself and becoming still, one can expand awareness. Surrounding the mental layer is the layer of intellect or intuition (Vigyanamaya Kosha). All learned skills and knowledge become stored in this layer. Every potential that has been enhanced during a lifetime is registered in this layer. When one reincarnates, he brings these potentials along as this layer wraps another body into which the soul has incarnated. The final layer is that of bliss or Ananda (Anandamaya Kosha). It is also known as the casual body.

The Chakra-Nadi system is integral part of the astral body or etheric body. The human spine forms an important axis around which all bodies are centered. In the human body, the spine not only enables the body to stand erect and supports the weight of the upper body, it also channels the nerves from the brain to various parts of the body. Every part in the physical body has an astral equivalent.

There are 72000 Nadis in the ethereal body. Nadis are the astral equivalent of the nerves in the physical body. Just like the nerves, Nadis form ganglia or intersections. Yogis mention 108 such locations where the Nadis cross each other. Amongst these, six are located along our spines and are considered the most important for humans. These locations where the Nadis intersect are generally channels of Universal energy. They have been experienced as circling vortices on the backside of the spine. As a result they are called as wheels or Cakras or Chakras. These wheels extend through each etheric layer mentioned (Koshas). Spine is the bridge that links us with the Universe.

Though there are hundreds of works available about the Chakra-Nadi system, I am making a brief mention about them here in order to have continuity. Consciousness is not a single entity. It is more like a spectrum. Its layers are not distinctly separate and they overlap. Let us look at the consciousness in the world that we live in. Gravitation is a reality in this world. We all have evolved under the field of gravity. We do not think much about it. We can feel a shock if we suddenly feel a change in it. For example, when an elevator suddenly goes down or when a plane jumps in height due to turbulence or during a roller coaster ride or going in a boat in a rough sea. That is when we can clearly sense the power of the gravitational pull. Under gravity, matter tends to organize itself based on density.

The more the mass, the more it gets pulled towards the center of gravity. Matter of lower density is farther out from the center. Thus a layered system forms. Solid is denser than a liquid in general. Amongst solids, different materials have different densities. The densest material is at the lowest level. The lightest matter is far removed from the center of gravity. A layered structure evolves due to density differences. If one watched the convection currents in a liquid (boiling is an example), heat causes density of the liquid to lower and the higher density liquid that is cooler drops down to the bottom of the vessel. It gets heated and its density drops. By this time the layer that went up has cooled and has increased in density. It comes down and so on. The cycle repeats itself and the convection process happens. Under gravity, matter tends to layer itself according to the density variation.

If one looked at the layers according to the density, solid is closest to the center of gravity. Then liquid layers settle on top of the solid layer. The last one is a gaseous layer. Beyond that is the vacuum of space. Our consciousness follows a similar order. If one considered human consciousness, being vertical with our spine being erect has elevated our consciousness to range from the solid level to the sky level. Consciousness planes correspond to the density layers – solid (Earth), liquid (Water), gas (air), space and beyond. We are grounded beings. Our natural state is to be on the ground, being supported by it and feeling home in it. We are also made up of liquid up to 70 percent. These two layers are referred to as elements. Most humans are in these two planes of consciousness and are comfortable there. This is what I call as the street level. We can exist and live at this level. However, because of our erect spine, we have been exposed to levels of consciousness that are lighter and closer to the Universal consciousness that is all pervading and where one senses nothing. The whole Universe seems to have nothing in which everything has manifested and has settled under the fields of gravity. The erect spine simply intersects the higher planes of consciousness.

In general, the earthly human beings have found comfort in mere existence and reproduction at the lower levels of consciousness. However, influence has happened in some humans from the higher planes of consciousness due to their interaction across the spine. Awareness of the higher planes of consciousness has been facilitated by the solar energy. Heat sustains life in this planet. Without sun's light and heat, life cannot survive at a complex level such as humans. Heat is associated with fire, a transformative element. In Sanskrit, fire element is known as Agni. If transformational level of consciousness influences someone, it gives an exposure to higher planes of consciousness. And humans have become aware of these planes of consciousness. One way of discovering them has been through inward focus. When we consciously experience something, we focus inwardly. If someone is asked to observe her breath cycles her mind will immediately turn inward.

Through inward focus, one can begin to observe more subtle

things. Through experiencing subtle things, one can reach deeper inside and begin to realize these planes of consciousness that are intersecting at different levels of the erect human spine.

It is these layers of higher consciousness that have enabled humans to possess capabilities that other beings do not. The ability to speak a language, being skilled, being able to think, becoming creative in arts, music, dance and so on, are a result of the higher planes of consciousness in humans. Though these planes of consciousness intersect the erect spine in every human, only some have managed to really explore them and derive benefit from them. The intersection planes correspond to physical organs in the human body. Just like the movement of energy is observed in matter in the form of waves, when consciousness expands in the different intersecting layers across the spine, humans experience different emotions and the corresponding physical organs respond. Both positive and negative emotions are sensed through their impact on the physical organs.

Love is sensed in one's heart. Shock causes heart to beat rapidly. Courage is linked to one's guts. Panic makes one queasy in the stomach. Stress causes neck to stiffen. When relaxed, one can speak clearly and calmly. Reproductive organs become excited when the consciousness plane corresponding to them feels energized. What one realizes through inner experience is that organs only act like musical instruments. They emit the final sounds while the music comes from the one who plays the instrument. These planes consciousness go by many names in different cultures. Yogis have sensed their presence deeply. They mention that these planes of consciousness are integral with the various layers (Koshas) of the etheric body that surrounds every being. Sensation in the organs corresponding to the different planes of consciousness happens when energy is directed though them either deliberately or unintentionally. Various emotions arise as a result. Some of these emotions have been needed for our survival – Fear, Anxiety, Affection, Anger etc. However, humans have the mental layer (Manomaya Kosha) where various memories and experiences become cumulative. These can lead to compulsive behavior and affect others.

These layers or planes of consciousness interact through the Nadis or Meridians that go along the spinal column. The locations where the Nadis cross each other and form ganglia are the ones where the various consciousness planes intersect the body. These locations are at various spots across the physical body and outside of it. I am using the physical body because that is the reference frame from which I can explain. We have the spine as our axis. Everything in a human body is oriented with respect to the spine. If our legs are taken away, we can still support our bodies with our spines. The arm and legs are mainly for physical motion. There are Nadi cross over junctions along the arms and legs as well. However, humans are strongly connected to the intersection planes along the vertical spine. Different endocrine glands and organs in the physical body that govern the aspects of reproduction, digestion, elimination, circulation, metabolism, protection, intuition etc. are influenced by these planes of intersection with the layers of consciousness. In yogic lore, these intersections are known as Chakras or Cakras. A chakra in many Indian languages means a wheel.

30 PLANES OF CONSCIOUSNESS

Let us return to our existence in a gravitational field. We have evolved under gravity. We do not fight it. We are comfortable with it. The surface of the earth is where we dwell and do not think much about gravity at all. The earth is spinning around its axis close to around 1100 miles per hour. But we have no realization of it at all. Everything seems static and stationary to us. At this level, being grounded is a very comforting feeling. It is where we would like to rest. When we rest, we sit down or lie down. We do not hang from our ceilings. We do not like to move or spend any energy when we are resting. After we have eaten a good meal, we like to rest and let the digestive process do its work. This is true especially after a heavy lunch. In many countries, they have a siesta time. This is when the digestive organs go to work. Blood flow is directed more towards the processes of digestion and elimination. In general, it is a time to be at rest and keep activities to the minimal. This is the basic state of our existence – eat, rest, digest, and eliminate. Many would love to wake up late in the morning and do nothing. Lying down flat on a bed or on the ground takes the least energy. Everything tries to reach the point of lowest energy. The river finds its way to the ocean due to the very reason. Under gravity, it tries to find its resting place. We do the same.

A good rest is refreshing. This is the seat of a consciousness plane where our existence as humans is based. This consciousness plane just touches a spot in our ethereal bodies that corresponds to the tip of our tailbones in the physical body. It is the foundation of our human existence. It is like the root for a tree. No tree can survive without its roots. And roots are in the ground. For stability, ground is very important, especially when we exist under gravity.

This state is basic existence. It is a state of rest. It is a state of digestion. At this stage, we resemble all the other animals, which do pretty much the same. Almost all animals, other than us, seem to be eating machines. They continuously look for food, consume it and rest to digest it. There is nothing else that interests them. There is no curiosity about what is around and why things are the way they are. The stars in the sky arouse no curiosity. Everything is guided by instinct. Every being feels individualistic and thinks only about its needs and survival. In humans, the mind has more capacity than the animals. For a mind that has no interest in the world around, other than for the self and its needs, this consciousness turns into what is termed as ego. In Sanskrit the word for it is "Aham Bhava", or Self-centeredness. A human dwelling at this level of consciousness does not have to be living in the jungle. Primitiveness is in the mind. Someone can be working in a modern city, earning a huge salary. Yet his life can be as mundane as that of a cow. He has no interest in any activities. He likes to eat, watch television and let others do the work. Even going to fetch water seems like an ordeal to him. On the other hand, a man living in a "primitive" tribe is active. He rests only when he needs to. He is very knowledgeable about his territory. He sharpens his weapons. He knows about the various animals in the region. He knows the various locations for resources like water. He is pretty much independent and content.

In yogic lore, this plane of consciousness is known as "Moola Adhara" (Basic foundation or support structure). Consciousness, like light, has a range or spectrum. The human consciousness starts at the level of the Moola Adhara. This is the seat of the ego, which relies entirely on the senses to orient itself. It is the consciousness of relative references. Everything appears simple and linear. Extremes appear real and separate. One sees himself distinctly separate from everything around. He goes entirely by his basic needs. Knowledge is a waste. He is content. If he suffers from anything, he blames others around him. At this level, one is almost like an animal. He defends his territory. He does not question. He cannot exist without an external identity. He avoids exploring unless he is pushed out. He simply believes and can easily be manipulated and misled. He thinks of himself as the sheep.

At the Moola Adhara center, three important Nadis come together in the ethereal body. The central one goes through vertically upwards and goes by the name Sushumna. There are two other Nadis that go by the names Ida and Pingala. They are also known as the Solar and Lunar Nadis or Hot and Cold. These two Nadis also meet at a point just outside the tip of the nose. Prana, or life force enters through each Nadi and exits each time we inhale and exhale. Yogis have noticed that when we breathe, air enters through only one nostril and exits through the same nostril for a certain period of time[8]. Then it switches to the other nostril. Prana does a corresponding action of entering and exiting through either the Ida or Pingala Nadi.

Outward looking existence relies on our ego, instincts and senses. If one turned his attention inward, this ego becomes life energy, which is called as "Kundalini". This life energy is denoted as feminine in the form of a coiled serpent. Kundalini remains dormant at this center of consciousness for humans. She is like a river being held by a dam. If the dam opens, the river will burst through. The gate at the Sushumna Nadi is closed for ordinary humans. This gate is kept closed by the force known as Ganesha. When Ganesha is invoked through proper meditation, Pranayama, yoga, mantra exercises, he allows the gate of the Sushumna Nadi to open. This sounds trivial. However, it can take many life cycles of effort.

Just existing alone is not enough for the individuals. Because the mortal body ends. It needs reproduce so that the species can renew itself. When Karma is involved, beings need a means to be born again. The next Consciousness plane of intersection corresponds to the reproductive organs. This goes by the name "Swadishtana". Life originated in water. Embryos form inside a liquid and grow in liquid until they are ready to separate and move about. Consciousness at this level is related to the water element. If the energy is intense in this plane, one can either become a great admirer of beauty or become a slave of sensual pleasure. Blockages in Nadis can cause the latter effect in people.

Most humans operate in the range of consciousness between these two Chakras. This is what I would call as the street level spirituality. One is controlled by emotions and identities. Through life's experience and Karma, humans want to see an end to their plight and suffering. Nothing is uniform in this world. Different beings operate at different consciousness levels and there is a constant interaction going on between them. At some point, some realize the need to go beyond mundane existence. This is the time of transformation. A small dent happens in their awareness and begins to drive a wedge. Such people realize they can help others or lead them. A burning desire dawns in their consciousness to know more. Mundane existence looks boring to them. They are now being influenced by the consciousness plane that intersects the solar plexus region of the spine. This is known as Manipuraka Chakra where transformation can take place. It is appropriately called as the Solar plexus region since Sun is an element that burns everything up. This is the entrance into the temple from the street. One is still drawn by the desire to remain or return to the street. This is the timberline demarcation beyond which going alone can be scary. Guides can help go up further towards the summit. Many still would miss the life at the base and return there. Some decide to move up and seek guides.

Guides who help the aspirants climb will now look for their preparedness. If one is heavy and slow or if one is really sick or handicapped, climbing now is not the right thing to do. One has to go back down, fully recover and return. Expedition gets harder beyond the timberline. One has to be disciplined, fit and be eager to go further. Just having the interest in not adequate. One is at the entrance of the temple. A person becomes a seeker at this stage. Until this level, he was a believer. Now he has questions and seeks guidance. The guide is not interested in narrating how things look from the summit. He wants the seeker to climb all the way and see for himself. Here too one has to be lucky. There are many who masquerade as guides. It is difficult to tell which one is the genuine guide who has been to the summit and really knows what he is capable of. Some believe they have become guides even after climbing a little bit more elevation and seen the summit from below.

A seeker has to make a firm decision. He cannot keep looking back. The goal must be to get to the summit, away from the force of gravity. Kundalini can ascend to each level of consciousness and operate between the Muladhara and the higher level. She does not go beyond that level because of any blockage.

As he climbs he can see birds flying freely, defying gravity. They flap their wings and use the air to float higher and higher without being influenced by gravity like he is. The bird only returns down to perch and that too it mostly stays away from the ground, on a tree branch or on a cliff. The consciousness plane at this level brings lighter feelings. It intersects the spine where the heart is. It corresponds to the air element. This center goes by the Sanskrit name "Anahata" which means unhurt or unbeaten. People whose Kundalini can rise up to this level become full of unconditional love. They spend their lifetime helping others. They forgive easily and work for the wellbeing of others.

When one reaches the summit, there are two views – one of the lands below and the other of the unlimited sky. At night, he can see the countless stars dotted across an endless expanse of cosmos. He is closer to it than someone at the base. He wants to fly freely from here, unbound by gravity. The view from here is something one cannot get at the base or below. One can turn around and look in all directions as far as the horizon. The whole world appears spectacular from this level. There is confidence, having reached the summit and he knows how to get there. There is no confusion anymore. There is clarity of vision. His expression becomes clear as a result. He has no hesitation to express what he is experiencing and what he describes is real. He does not mince his words. The plane of consciousness corresponding to this state intersects the spine near the throat. People in whom the Kundalini ascends to this level of consciousness are great orators, writers, composers and performers. They somehow appear possessed and what they deliver is inspiring. The gateway for this consciousness plane is known as "Vishuddhi" Chakra.

Beyond the summit, it is physically not possible to fly up or climb any higher. But one can enter the meta-physical realm. Everything is an experience. All experience happens in our vision. However, ordinary mortals will have to imagine or hallucinate an experience that they have not had before. A yogi who goes beyond the summit now acquires a capability where he does not have to go physically to any place to experience it. He can be at the base of the mountain and know the entire experience of being at the summit. Or vice versa. He has transcended the entire physical approach and has now is at the entrance of the inner sanctum. This plane of consciousness does not intersect the spine. It is above it and inside the head, which is the seat of knowledge. The gateway corresponding to this level of consciousness is known as Agnya Chakra. This is also known as the "Third eye" and corresponds to the physical location where the pineal gland is situated. By making the pineal gland secret through yogic exercise, a yogi can make every cell in his body feel blissful.

The third eye is not physically an eye. We use the word eye to denote it because we do not have any other word in our language. It definitely is associated with a vision that can make any experience real. A yogi who has the Kundalini rising up to the Agnya Chakra acquires tremendous power according to Patanjali's Yoga Sutra. His intuitive power is so immense that he knows the question even before it is asked. He can now sense the astral layers in everything. He can guide others. This Chakra is also known as "Kutasta Chaitanya" or "Krishna Consciousness" or "Christ Consciousness". Yogis mention that we only utilize a small percentage of brainpower. According to them, when one's Agnya Chakra is activated, his brainpower reaches almost 100 percent. Anyone who reaches this level of consciousness can have immense power hold over others. If he so desires, the world would submit to him. However, such an act can trigger the buried ego to come out with full force in some, destroying him and his followers. One only wants to guide at this stage and not lead. Leading has its pitfalls.

Brain however is a limited organ. What connects an individual to the Universe is something above the brain. The Sushumna Nadi goes beyond the Pineal gland and reaches a spot above the crown of the head. This spot is where the Nadi ends. If the Nadi is open all the way up to this spot, Kundalini will ascend unhindered up to this spot and merge with the Universe. It is known as the seat of Shiva, which is Universal Consciousness. Manifestation separates the Shakti or Kundalini from Shiva. We, the manifested, form the bridge that links the two. We humans have the means to realize that union. When Shakti unites with Shiva, it is known as Yog or Yoga.

In many cultures this union goes by different names. In the Indian traditions, one who experiences this union is known as the Brahman. The meaning for Brahman is one who is born again. Everyone is born in a physical body. The one who reaches the Universal Consciousness, awakens in it and it is like another birth. Every birth comes with a consciousness.

Human birth happens at the Muladhara (Root) level of consciousness. But humans have the potential to reach the higher level of consciousness by using their bodies and minds. This birth is also known as the "Virgin Birth" where no physical union is involved. It is beyond mind and body. The opening of the Sushumna Nadi is described also in other traditions in different ways – The opening of the ocean to make way for Moses to lead the Israelites to the Promised Land is an example.

When Kundalini unites with Shiva Consciousness above the crown, ego is completely destroyed. The ascendance from the Agnya Chakra to the crown needs a Guru's activation. A guru touches his disciple symbolically to make this union happen in his disciple. This is known in Sanskrit as Shaktipat. The guru does not give this blessing to every disciple who has reached the level of the Agnya Chakra. Ego is still present at this level and it can turn one into a monster because of the power associated with this level of consciousness. This is the seat of the inner sanctum, or the deity or Universal Consciousness. It is the Lingam that has been depicted as penetrating through the vulva inside the Garbha Griha or the womb. This union is cosmic and does not belong to the world of matter, which is manifest. Here manifestation has dissolved into the unmanifest.

The Lingam, which is described as the phallus, has even a deeper meaning than that. It is an ellipsoidal shape and the primordial manifestation or dissolution of the manifest has been realized in the form of an ellipsoid by the yogis. They call this shape as the Lingam. The union of Shiva and Shakti at the crown of one's head goes by many names – Self Realization, Nirvana, Bodhi-Sattva, Satori, Samadhi, Enlightenment etc. A yogi, who achieves this state, does not keep the Kundalini merged at all times with the Universal Consciousness. He directs her usually to the heart Chakra. He can now guide others with unconditional love and compassion. His entire life now becomes a meditative process. Everything he does happens in his full consciousness. His awareness has expanded beyond his body. His intuition is strong and he can sense everything around him. He does not need the five senses to experience reality. And the reality he experiences does not have to be local.

There are yogis who decide to make the union permanent and leave their bodies for good. They have no more need to be born in a body again to learn awareness. They are aware even without a body at this stage. By merging entirely with the Universal Consciousness, they remain alive and aware, independent of time or any dimension. They are known as the immortals. The others remain for the simple reason to help others and guide them through the same pathways that they were guided through.

I started describing about the religion called Hinduism at the beginning. Now I have reached the very essence of it, where the name Hinduism has become irrelevant. Religion is only the starting point. The essence is the same and is Universal. Many people who call themselves as Hindus have very scant information about the core essence of their system. What one sees as Hinduism is only what is visible at the street level. Even if one's body goes through the corridors of the temple and goes close to the inner sanctum, the mind can still be at the street level. Everything has been set up to help the mind walk in from the street into the temple.

Humans come in many colors. Each one of us is a painting where various colors have been tossed in and the outcome is a unique artwork. How one mixes up the paint, the color tones and the patterns that arise from the brush stroke determine how good or bad a painting looks. In reality we are the canvas on which the painting is done. But many get drawn to the painting. Paintings do fall into categories even though each one of them is unique. One can have an oil painting, watercolor, impression, abstract and so on. The quality of the work depends upon the skill and creativity of the artist. In the Hindu systems, humans have been classified into four such colors and one more, which is outside of the classification.

31 COLORS

It is not enough if I do not mention about one of the critical aspects of the Hindu social structures. When European explorers set foot in the Indian sub-continent, in addition to the wealth and empires, they observed a unique social structure. The Portuguese called it as the caste system because they found the structure to be rigid. When a principle is misinterpreted and abused to enhance power and control over others, a society falls into a dark age. This system had become well entrenched even before the time of Buddha, who simply decided to have a new start, negating all the aspects that had become the controlling tool at the hands of some who had corrupted the system. The real meaning of it has been ignored. What is known today is what it has become due to manipulation and control of others.

The planes of consciousness that intersect the spine have different influences on each individual. Three qualities emerge within each individual due to the varying influence of the consciousness planes. These qualities dominate different individuals based on his or her awareness and spiritual development. Every consciousness plane has both positive and negative influences. Based on the choice every individual makes at each instant in life, these influences begin to build up within and accumulate. In the long run the accumulated influence begins to dominate one's vision and approach towards the world around.

For example, according to the yogic traditions, human consciousness ranges from mere animal like existence to the level of an exalted seer. Most humans exist under the influence of the two consciousness planes corresponding to the earth (root) and water (sacral) elements. One can exist at these levels and make good choices. Such choices help an individual easily become aware of the higher levels of consciousness and make the choice to pursue them. Such individuals are very sincere, devout, humble, receptive, innocent and trusting. It is almost like a child's nature. It is the characteristic of a simpleton. At this level one is vulnerable to manipulation by others. However, if one manages to survive without any exploitation, such an individual will radiate Divine purity from within without having to attempt anything. Exposure and awareness of the higher planes of consciousness will happen on their own. In the real world where life is shared with others, this rarely happens. Modern world has nearly destroyed the chances of pure development in any individual. One has to seek refuge in mountains and caves today to experience that simple existence which is the starting point.

In the civilized world, one always gets pushed and shoved around by others. One cannot remain innocent like the squirrel in the middle of the road. It will be trampled and run over. This brings survival instincts to awaken where one has to push and shove others to get through daily life. The natural home has now become the street. In the street, there is no time to sit and ponder about the purpose of life. When there is no time to look inward and look at oneself, the choices one makes tend towards selfishness. Everyone is for himself. One only looks ahead and never behind. One is constantly watching others and spends all the time adjusting his position to avoid running into them or get run over by them. This choice makes life even harder. One begins to plunge into the darkness of ignorance. There is no looking at oneself in the mirror. It is always others who are out to destroy oneself. The mind begins act like a predatory animal, ready to fight others for its share. Poor choices make karmic burden to increase. In Sanskrit, this quality is known as Tamas or darkness of ignorance.

A world influenced by Tamas spends little time feeling bad about exploiting others. The whole world and beyond are for exploitation.

Everything appears powerless and can be brought under control. People can easily be turned against each other. The same emotions that can be gateways to higher dimension can now be turned around to create more fear and enemies. Awareness or appreciation of higher dimensions becomes irrelevant. Interpretation becomes dominant over understanding.

Societies made up of individuals who are influenced by any dogma can have a tremendous impact on the world. Germany under the Nazis became one such society. There are many such instances in world history where collective influence turned negative and affected the world enormously. Even under such influence, there always individuals who manage to resist it and fight it. The reason why individuals exist is because all cannot be influenced to the same extent. There is always a random variation in influence. Individuals provide the diversity needed to stem a strong influence from anything. Usually they start out as a minority and then over time, manage to gain strength. In Sanskrit, this quality is known as Rajas. Rajasic quality always has the spirit of rebellion in it. It is influenced by the fire element of consciousness. The sun always dispels the darkness each morning. Every night is always ended by the dawn of light. Due to the cyclical nature of the universe, one finds ages that plunge beings into the darkness of ignorance and suffering and the dawn of awakening.

Once awakening happens, higher planes of consciousness begin to influence. This can take individuals to the most exalted state of becoming the Brahman, the enlightened. Such a person carries the same irradiance of purity, innocence, light heartedness, compassion, humbleness and respect as the simpleton. However, the enlightened person cannot be exploited because he or she is aware of everything and know the intention of others. They can completely manage to deflect any negative influence away and help those who are manipulated. They do not exploit anyone because they have completely ridden themselves of ego. In Sanskrit, such a quality is known as Sattva.

Tamas, Rajas and Sattva are the three qualities that arise due to the choices made by individuals at every instant of their lives.

Different individuals carry these qualities to varying extents. And their nature and behavior depends upon which quality dominates their minds depending upon the cumulative experience over many life times and circumstances. People with similar tendencies tend to gravitate towards each other. Beings with similar tendencies also tend to be born in societies made up of individuals dominated by similar qualities.

These qualities also tend to dominate the world in a cyclical fashion, each one having the strongest influence over a duration of time. In Sanskrit, such time periods are known as Yuga (or era). There are four such Yugas according to the ancient traditions. Kali Yuga is one where Tamas dominates with very minimal influence from Rajas and Sattva qualities. Treat Yuga is one in which Tamas and Rajas qualities dominate. In Dwapara Yuga, Sattvic qualities begin to influence more and Tamas is almost negligible. Finally under Satya Yuga, only Sattva quality remains. The beings that exist during this era are enlightened ones, sharing the world in peace and amity. The world goes through these four eras in a cyclical fashion. Kali Yuga is the age of exploitation. Ignorance dominates the mindset. One relies entirely on outward looking perspective of the world, brought about by the senses. Individuals with Sattvic qualities are rare.

Likewise, individuals dominated by Tamas are denoted by the term Shudra (pronounced as Shoo Dra). The majority of people in this world today would fit this description. There is nothing derogatory about being a Shudra. It is simply a quality that influences one's outlook of the world around. It is also the sign of the time period in which we exist. Shudra tendency is to be materialistic and pleasure loving. There is no interest to feel for others. Selfishness dominates the mind. It does not matter if one is rich or poor. The same attitude can be present in an individual dominated by the Shudra tendency. This mindset looks at the world as something to be dominated and exploited. It interprets anything to suit its needs and justifies its actions by using technicalities. It has

no sense of shame or feelings of guilt. When cornered, it always blames others for what it has become.

Though the world is dominated by Shudra tendencies during the Kali Yuga, there are always beings under the influence of the higher dimensions even during this time. They too exploit the world, but they carry a feeling of guilt in the corner of their minds. They sometimes give and help. However, they are still influenced by the Tamas quality. Such individuals are known as Vaisya. There is some awareness about higher dimensions and the need to look inwards in such people. But they are still drawn towards selfishness. Both the Tamas and Vaisya nature belong to the street. At this level religions are rigid and are used to exploit others. They do not see any other purpose behind religions. They see others with different beliefs as threatening and competing.

And there are individuals who realize that the world does not offer them the satisfaction that they are looking for. Money does not make them happy. They get tired of comfort and luxury. They feel deep inside themselves that their lives are not meant for mundane existence. There is something in them that is constantly pushing them to seek something beyond ordinary existence. These people want to do something and contribute something. They become the explorers and love venturing into the unknown. They are curious about the world around and what it offers. They love climbing peaks, risking their lives. They love nature and seek time in nature. They can lead others who belong to the Tamas and Vaisya nature. They have a better awareness about the world. However, they are at the crossroads. The material world still attracts them. Once in a while they plunge into the darkness and return. They regret their actions and choices. These are the ones that start showing interest in higher dimensions and want someone to guide them.

In Sanskrit, such persons are known as Kshatriya. A Kshatriya also means one who is a warrior. It has been wrongly interpreted by the Tamas dominated society and now there are classes of people in India who proudly call themselves as belonging to the Kshatriya caste. A true warrior has to be physically fit. He has to be disciplined and alert. He has to know his enemies and be ready to face them. He also must know those he has to protect. That is a true Kshatriya. One who leaves the street and enters the temple is a Kshatriya. His enemies are internal. All his tendencies, temptations and undesired habits appear powerful and strong at this stage. They are ready to fight him, defeat him and take him back to the street from where he came. A true Kshatriya is the spiritual seeker. He has reached the timberline and knows now that a fall from this altitude can be hard. If he seeks guidance, then he can climb higher.

A seeker, who receives guidance and follows the spiritual training given by his master, reaches the stage of enlightenment. His Nadis become clear of blockages. His Chakras become balanced. Kundalini arises from his root Chakra and ascends to his Crown where he is able to connect to the Universal consciousness. At this stage, he realizes the Brahma or the Universe within himself and outside. He is known as the twice born or the Brahman. In Kali Yuga, such Brahmans are rare. In Satya Yuga, the world is made up of Brahmans.

Thus the three qualities of Tamas, Rajas and Sattva decide how the world of individuals shapes up and how their influences changes within individuals as well as with time. The four classes of people mentioned is a result of which of these three qualities dominate them. In Sanskrit these four classes are known as Varna, or Color. It has nothing to do with physical colors. People influenced by Tamas, have misinterpreted this to mean skin color. These colors are those of the consciousness planes that influence the different qualities that arise due to individual choices.

At the street level, Varna or the Caste system has led to the exploitation of humans in India. Those who have gone beyond religions do not exercise any such beliefs. To them everyone is Divine and carries the same Universal spirit within. The street is a good starting point. However one must strive to become more aware and go beyond the street. The various scriptures and paths in Hindu systems point to the same thing – move from Tamas to Sattva. There is a famous Sanskrit prayer that asks for being guided from darkness to light, from untruth to truth, and from mortality to the immortality of unlimited and everlasting awareness.

32 THE MANY PATHS

There are innumerable paths towards the Universal Consciousness. If anyone asks where it is, it resembles the fish asking where water is and whether anyone has seen it. We are a negligible manifestation of it. It is called by many names. God is the most prevalent name. At the street level, such a name is all right. As one ascends to higher elevations or enters deeper towards the inner sanctum, names lose their meaning. One cannot describe the beauty he sees from the summit in words. It is an experience that everyone has to go through for himself. What is mentioned as Heaven at the street level is as real as Santa Claus bringing gifts during the middle of the night. What is mentioned as Hell is as real as a horror movie being screened. These are relative terms. In a dualistic world experienced at the street level, Heaven and Hell seem like two places distinctly apart.

Once one leaves the street and enters the temple or crosses the level of the timberline, relativistic perception begins to diminish. Senses begin to withdraw. Stillness is more appealing. Space and time begin to lose their meaning. Anyone who has entered that dimension does not want to come back down. There is more to know and explore and each step forward is more exciting than the previous one. Just like the world of mentally ill where the doctor appears abnormal, what the yogis and seekers mention appear strange and not of this world. Yogis are left to themselves. They are walking corpses as far as "normal" humans are concerned. Yogis take up that pursuit by performing their own funeral rites. After that they are known as wandering Sadhus who drop their birth names, give up all bonds with families and friends, and move on. They wander in order to eliminate attachment to places. The mind always feels nostalgic. Even the gurus remain with no attachment to their disciples. They are only there to guide. Once the disciple gets the same enlightenment as the guru, he is done. He can now go on his own and continue his practice. The guru is always respected and revered. But no hurt feelings remain.

There are many ways in which one reaches this state. The Universe is diverse. It is its nature. Therefore the paths to the Universe can also be diverse. Everything simply happens in the Universe. Similarity exists in manifestation and events. Evolution is a natural process. It did not start once the scientists discovered it. It has been going on from time immemorial. Evolution also happens at the consciousness level. There are many shades of consciousness and through each layer of it, the Universe looks different. White light when passed through a prism, splits into different colors ranging from red to violet. If we could sense only some of those colors, our perception of light would only be made up of those colors. It would need more introspection and understanding to realize that there is something called white light that covers all the colors that appear separate. Those who see the world through the red color filter might feel superior to those who view the world through the green filter. But what is important is the process of viewing and not the color itself. The process of viewing is an inner experience and through that one realizes that the entire spectrum is made up of one white light. And light itself is only a small band of a much larger spectrum known as the electro-magnetic waves.

The spiritual paths across India took the approach of focusing on the experience rather than the individual paths themselves. Each path is like the filter through which the Universe is viewed. Each individual has his own natural inclinations and tendencies. Based on his state of mind and inclinations, he might like to follow one path instead of the other. However, even if there is a path that is available to him, he can choose not to go through it at all and remain where he is. One has to have the freedom to pursue anything entirely out of his own will and interest. That step is taken when one does not like the way his life experiences are turning out. He cannot find a way out and everything becomes a suffering to him. Dissatisfaction sets in. This is the stage one tries to escape from. Some try negative methods like ending their lives or fall into mental sickness. Before reaching that threshold, if one thinks and looks for a way out, he will always find one. This is why the world always has had spiritual guides and religion. These are outlets for humans to find a way out of their inner suffering.

Suffering might be undesirable. But all suffering is one's own making. Physical suffering can be healed. But real suffering happens in the mind. What affects the mind, affects the body and the two begin to suffer even more. Suffering is simply a trigger for looking inward. At some point people begin to look inward. It is like pain in the body. Pain is not for making one suffer. It is to prevent a person from over exerting and hurting himself more. One does not exert the hurt part of the body and treats it in order to recover. Suffering causes one to stop and seek a relief. In India millions of people flock to temples and religious gatherings. Religious leaders have mass following. Everyone thinks in a simplistic way in order to resolve their issues that could range from not getting a job, not getting married, not having a child, not making a profit, not making friends and so on. People flock to pilgrimage centers in millions. Many have a list of wishes to seek. Many chant mantras to find remedies to problems that involve others. Some turn to philosophy and try to find solace in them.

Out of the many, some turn deeply inward and they find that all suffering has become external. They find something deep inside, which appears unaffected by everything on the outside. Then things they see around themselves begin to make sense. They realize the message from everything around – the mountains, the rivers, the homes, the streets, the animals, the stars and people. And they find these messages depicted in different ways – in the form of mythology, poetry, scriptures and writings. Going through them draws them more inward and they begin to discover more insight. They do not find many around them who are at the same level of vision. They realize that those with similar frequency of thought and ideals are far and few in number. But they seek the company of such peers.

Most Hindu systems emphasize on reincarnation of the soul and the belief in karma. When one dies, he returns when the right conditions for his life experiences and potential are met. He continues from there. Because of the infinite degrees of freedom, he can keep going in circles if he does not realize the purpose of his being. There always arises a point where the individual decides to go even higher and deeper. This is when he seeks guidance. If he prepares himself properly, guidance always comes. Based on his nature, tendencies and inclinations, there is a path open to him. If he followed that path sincerely, he will reach the summit along that path with the help of his guide. There is no such thing as a superior path. Every path has emerged due to the walking of many with similar capabilities. They made the path happen by walking on it. In India the paths are many, even though they all have been clubbed into a single system called Hinduism. That may be all right at the street level. Having brought the reader somewhat deeper, I am going to describe some paths that are used by many to reach the spiritual summit across India.

Ancient India is associated with the age of sages or rishis. Many of these sages appear in Indian mythology regularly. There was dense vegetation and population was scant during their times. Tribal societies existed. The entire language of Sanskrit is known as the language of the Gods ("Deva Bhasha"). Sanskrit language is said to have evolved in the consciousness of sages during deep meditation. The syllables, symbols and script appeared in their vision. They composed many mantras and chants in praise of Deities that were orally propagated through generations. The mantras had an outward meaning. But the pronunciation of the syllables triggered subtle inner vibrations. Their method of worship involved fire rituals and sacrifices (known as "Homa" and "Yagnya"). This is known as the "Nigama" system. Ancient India had the Nigama system prevalent across the land. Advances in spiritual practices were developed during this time. Modern day Hindu astrology can be dated back to this time period.

In Tantric system different methodologies are used to attain spiritual enlightenment. Shiva is mentioned as Bhairava, the Tantric master. Unlike the Nigama system where offerings were made to ethereal deities through fire sacrifices, drinking of the Soma elixir and not involving centers or temples, the Tantric system uses physical world for spiritual advancement. In this system, pilgrimage is important. So are temples, deities, mantras, Yantras and rituals. Most of what we see today in contemporary Hindu religions traces their origin back to Tantra. There are different pathways in the Tantric system itself.

Spiritual awakening is achieved by the manipulation of Shakti (or energy). Therefore Tantra is also known as Shakti Sadhana (practice)[9]. Tantric practitioners have understood the subtle characteristics in everything around – sounds, colors, geometry, animals, herbs, minerals, trees, rivers, mountains etc. and have used them to awaken the Divine energy within. They have discovered the vibrations in these objects relate to various energy centers in the human body. Tantric approach has been responsible for the development of yoga, medicine (Ayurveda), Alchemy and Astrology.

Tantra became quite prevalent across certain regions of the sub-continent. Everything in Tantra has to be pursued under the guidance of a master. Fire as a transformational element is central to the Tantric practice. Based on the astrological chart for each individual, the appropriate kind of materials for a ritual, the proper Mudras (gestures) and procedures were prescribed by an adept. Mimicking any of the rituals can be ineffective or harmful. Many charlatans thrived using Tantric practices to cast spells, black magic etc. which brought a bad name for the system. The intentions of the practitioner are extremely crucial. Since Tantra uses material to achieve the goal of enlightenment, the same material can be used for selfish purposes. The science has been kept secretive because of the danger of misuse. Tantric gurus make their appearances horrifying sometimes to repel the curious seekers. Getting them to reveal anything is extremely difficult.

One has to be able to control his mind in order to be ready to receive guidance. Tantra has been associated with magic and miracles. This was done to filter out true seekers. Anyone who was attracted to magic was distracted away. The true aspirant looked beyond that and the master was ready to teach him beyond the miracles. However, those aspects have been abused by many who learned them and used them to control others. Tantra as well as other traditions prevalent in India is known as "Agama" systems, which involve temples, deities and rituals.

Shiva following has been one of the most native traditions of India. Shiva, depicted as a yogi has been known for thousands of years Shiva has been worshipped as far as Central Asia in the past. When Buddhism began to spread across Northern parts of India, Shiva following (Shaivism) emerged in a big way in the Southern part of India. The emperors in the peninsular India became staunch worshippers of Shiva and built massive temples that still stand today. Buddhism had brought monastic tradition. The Hindu equivalent emerged under the leadership of Sankaracharya.

Following Vishnu (Vaishnavism) gained momentum around the same time period. Vishnu worship did not follow the rigid discipline of Shaivism. Vaishnavism is rooted in the avatars of Vishnu and devotion towards Him. Many saints emerged in Southern India that won the royal patronage. Massive temples were built for Vishnu in many places. Shiva and Vishnu following became two predominant pillars of new age Hinduism. The two cults engaged in debates and tried to win royal patronage. At the same time, they also pushed Buddhism and Jainism to the fringes. These being atheistic in principle, lost out to Shaivism and Vaishnavism as these cults developed public appeal and regal support. They gained popularity due to mythology and epics, as well as becoming less abstract. People at the street level simply cannot take up something abstract and sit down to meditate. They are like children from a spiritual standpoint. Children can only be taught through playing. Shaivism and Vaishnavism have the necessary elements that appeal to the spiritual children of the land. In addition, many local deities were added and integrated to bring more people under the fold.

Shaivism and Vaishnavism also included devotional aspects (Bhakti). These branches completely negated Sanskrit and the scriptures in it. Instead scriptures and anthologies in local vernacular languages were favored. This happened especially in Southern India.

The arrival of Turks and Mongols changed the landscape in Northern India. These were tribesmen from Central Asia who had take up Islam as their religion. They simply could not comprehend the diverse systems prevalent across the land. They were interested in establishing their power and expanding their territory more than anything else. They had to employ the natives of the land in their armies and administration. Many of the Muslim Sultans became native to the land themselves. Most of them did not offset the local beliefs and traditions. Some eagerly invited people of other religions to their courts to learn more about them. Some even gave alms and charity to Hindu temples. Northern India saw an integration of the Turko-Persian system and the native traditions over time. Temple architecture resembled the Persian monuments. Sculpture along the temple walls and perimeter were abandoned. Marble became one of the main building materials in the Hindu temples across Northern India. The devotion movement (Bhakti) caught on, where rituals and orthodox methods were abandoned. Singing and dancing were integral part of the devotion movement.

Southern India managed to keep the old traditions somewhat alive. The original Tantric traditions of temple building (Agama Shastra) have been retained in the Southern part of the land more. Backwardness had crept due to frequent wars and conflicts across the land. Empires collapsed and stability was affected. The land had entered a period of darkness when colonial powers arrived. The British managed to capture all of India within a period of a hundred years and ruled the land for another century and a half. During that time period, the Indian subcontinent underwent more changes and adjustments. The British settled themselves in the land and began to study the ancient traditions and social structure of the land. Some British men interacted with yogis. Some became disciples of yogis and moved into the mountains to meditate. The Asiatic Society was formed in Calcutta under Alexander Cunningham.

Archeology department focused on India was started by the British. The work done by the archeologists helped unearth hitherto unknown Harappan civilization. Europeans arrived in India to learn Sanskrit and translate the many scriptures and epics. India as the land of yogis was known. India emerged independent in 1947 and has been inching its way towards economic progress. Despite all the various influences upon the land, India still has managed to keep its ancient traditions alive. This has been possible by the system of self-realized gurus and their disciples. The rest have been at the street level of spiritualism. Things have been deliberately kept that way. The one who seeks will find what he needs. When he discovers himself, he will only work for the good of others. One has to become ready in order to receive. We do not hand over the car keys to our pre-teen children and do not trust the teenage drivers. We know that they are not ready to drive off on their own. The same applies for spiritual development.

33 FAITH AND INTUITION

Evolution has been going on for millions of years. Planets have been going around the stars for billions of years. There has been no external control to any of these processes. There is something called natural tendency along which everything proceeds. Everything in the Universe has its own natural tendency. There is no such thing as limitedness. The eagle does not have hands. We cannot fly by ourselves. The dog cannot swim like a dolphin. A dolphin cannot walk on the land like a penguin. Everything operates within its own realm where its needs are met. Everything is learned in a natural way. Lions learn to hunt by watching other lions. They make mistakes at the beginning. But experience improves their skills. Domesticated animals lack the skills to survive in the wild, which is their natural domain. Children learn to speak by watching and mimicking others. Such skills arise out of necessity for survival. All the learning in nature happens by the process of intuition.

Intuition does not involve any analytical methods. It relies on one's capability to sense. Some people are said to have musical "sense". They pick up their capability to play music just by listening. Some people are called as sharp shooters. They do not calculate anything. They just aim and shoot, right on a target that can be moving. Some people can do incredible things in sports that have never been done before. Some can come up with prodigious work in music or dance or arts. Famous sculptors like Michael Angelo simply saw the final form they were going to sculpt when they saw the marble piece the first time. Geniuses simply see what they create. Some math prodigies see a solution just by looking at a problem, however complex it might be. If one asks them about how they do what they do, they have no idea. Somehow things appear to them. They are able to delve into the depths of their intuition and there they find incredibly creative ideas to express in their own ways.

The best learning happens by intuitive methods. In many Eastern cultures including India, teaching is done by intuitive methods. In India, classical music is taught that way even today. Part of the teaching involves relying on one's memory. Nothing is explained. One simply learns by repetition. It becomes an automatic, ingrained aspect in the individual and like a language, expresses itself without any hindrance. Amendments and improvements happen slowly and in small increments. Nothing is done drastically. It is well known that children who take to learning music at a very young age become very good in mathematics. Math and analytical subjects are associated with left-brain while intuitive aspects like music and art are right brain activities. It sounds paradoxical when one learns a right brain activity like music, it enhances the left-brain skill in mathematics. The real reason is that math is like music. If one developed a music skill at an early age, it sets up a deep intuitive capability in a person and that in turn makes learning much easier, including math.

Analytical approach has been in vogue for the past two thousand years in Europe and that has come to dominate the world in its quest for knowledge. It has shaped the culture of the people in the Western world in all aspects. Analytical or left brained activity is done with the conscious mind. This needs careful recording of everything, a structured and compartmentalized approach towards learning. Western classical music is taught by writing the notes down and reading the notes while playing instruments or singing. There is nothing inferior in this approach. It helps many reproduce a great work done by someone in the past. Everything has to be broken down into simple steps and one relies on references in that system. One cannot perceive the world without a point of origin. Everything has to be catalogued and recorded in an order. This method has its advantages and it has helped modern science and technology to progress to where it is today. It helps the common man gain access to many things that would otherwise would be esoteric. Common man relies on his conscious mind and cannot be creative. Geniuses rely on intuition entirely. And they create incredible things and shift the world in new directions. Analytical approach has been very methodical in everything. It cannot delve on subjects that cannot be proved. This approach sees humans as above nature and there is a desire to control everything after understanding how it works.

In the Hindu system, the left-brain based approach is considered masculine. The right brained approach is feminine which is more intuition based, relying on sensing and feeling. This sees humans as a part of nature and not above it. When a religion becomes structured, based on an analytical approach, its true purpose gets lost. It creates hierarchy and ranked order. It leads to interpretation rather than understanding. Restrictions arise.

In the intuition-based approach, a religion is a realm in which everyone gets an exposure until an internal trigger happens in some people in a natural way. Rules or order exists at the fundamental level. Randomness operates on top of this fundamental structure. For example, if one took two saplings belonging to the same species of trees, they contain the same type of DNA in them. Yet their branches and leaves can grow in every random way. Their growth and survival process alone rely on the fundamental structure of their DNA. As far their response to the randomly varying surrounding conditions, no restrictions are imposed. The ancient religious systems of the world followed the same approach.

The greatest thoughts, ideas and discoveries in this world have arisen out of intuition. They happened suddenly and profound truths were revealed at an instant.

The fundamental essence or structure of the intuition-based approach is to rely on senses and emotions. In order to start from a limited physical realm and reach into the unlimited Universe, one has to rely on the natural inclinations, intuition, senses and emotions. Even the greatest scientist, who knows all about reproduction process, has to fall in love with someone. He cannot be analyzing the process when he is in love. Falling in love is the starting point that results in the next generation. Likewise, if one were to link and unite with the Universe, devotion becomes an extremely important starting point. In Sanskrit, the equivalent word is "Bhakti". Bhakti is not merely devotion in the real sense. It is a mix of several aspects that include devotion, sincerity, faith, belief, love and respect. One approaches the unlimited Universe through the gate of Bhakti. There is no other way available for humans.

Martin Luther King once said that faith is like taking a step even if there is no staircase. One has to have unshakeable faith in his pursuit of spiritual awakening. There is a story of a seeker who had such a faith. He was a staunch devotee of Abhirami, a form of Shakti. He had so much faith in his Divine mother that he would enter a state of stillness whenever he was near the inner sanctum of the Abhirami temple. One day the king arrived to offer his respect and prayer to mother Abhirami. When a king comes, everything gets cleared away. His guards found this seeker sitting in deep meditation and not moving. The king was curious about this man who had no respect or regard for him. Everyone was afraid of what would happen.

The king asked the seeker about the phase of the moon for that day. On that day, it so happened it was new moon. The seeker was in such bliss that he saw tremendous light in his vision. He simply uttered that it was a full moon. The king was surprised. He felt he was talking to a mad man who had no respect for him. When he asked him again the same question, the seeker replied the same answer. The king was annoyed by this arrogant answer. He had his guards take the mad man away and imprisoned. In addition he declared that if the seeker does not prove that it was a full moon day, he would be put to death.

The seeker was in ecstasy, laughing in joy, singing in praise of the Divine mother when he was chained and held in the prison. The evening came and everyone assembled to see the outcome. The seeker was brought in chain. The king sat on a throne. The seeker's friends asked for mercy but the king wouldn't relent. Night came. Stars filled the dark sky and the moon was nowhere to be seen. The king asked the seeker to answer one final time whether it was a full moon or a new moon. The seeker, still in ecstasy replied his mother would make it happen. The king laughed and ordered that if the full moon did not arise within the next hour, the seeker would be put to death for insulting him. The seeker began to sing in ecstasy. He showed absolutely no fear of dying. People had given up hope. The time arrived. The swordsmen were brought in to behead the seeker who kept singing in praise of his Divine mother. He suddenly looked up and smiled in absolute joy. The sky began to dazzle with brilliant light. It was blinding to everyone's eyes. The chains fell off from the seeker. In their place a huge garland decorated his neck. The king realized his mistake. When the brilliant light subsided, he fell at the feet of the seeker and sought his forgiveness. So goes the story. Unshakeable faith can be miraculous.

If one needs to become a true seeker, his faith has to be as strong as mentioned in the story above. In order to become a seeker, one needs to believe first. Belief leads to faith. Faith leads to sincerity. Sincerity leads to discipline. One does not become arrogant because he has progressed much compared to others. His love for others and humbleness have to remain intense all the time. Only then guidance arrives. A mother does not control her child. She cares for it. She does not act arrogant towards her children because they are small and depend on her. She lives for them. Spiritual quest has to be based on a similar footing. One cannot make any progress without the basic ingredients of humbleness, unconditional love, respect, faith and devotion. Any pursuit devoid of these elements is like admiring a blank wall. It does not lead to anything. The only way and the simplest way to create that kind of mindset is to have a God in the human form who can romance, play, fight wars to protect His believers and offer wisdom when needed. The most advanced method can start out on a very simple way. One can get a PhD sometime. The starting point always is the preschool. We perceive everything in human terms. Therefore there is nothing wrong in taking everything from that reference frame and building on it. Advancement will happen on its own. Such an approach will avoid arrogance and the urge to control others and nature. It is a slow approach. But it always works in the long run. The road to wisdom starts at a very simple level. One does not achieve spiritual progress in reality. All one does is become aware of his spiritual nature, which is unlimited in every way.

34 THE ESSENCE

By seeing lemon juice in a vessel, one cannot tell how exactly the lemon looked before the juice was extracted. What matters is the juice and the pulp has been discarded. The juice is the essence one extracts from the lemon. This is what is being digested by the body once it is consumed. It has the necessary elements (vitamins, anti-oxidants etc.) that the body can benefit from.

Likewise, if one managed to get into the essence of the Hindu religions, their external shape and appearance become irrelevant. The essence of most of these religions is the same. They have the elements that will benefit the human spirituality. All one has to do is to imbibe them in his daily aspects of life. The environment will begin to operate in subtle ways in order to induce an awakening. The true essence is to use the physical body and environment to transcend into a cosmic realm.

Encountering Hindu religions is like walking into wild place filled with various fruit trees. They might appear haphazardly arranged. Many simply eat the fruits, enjoy the taste of the flesh and throw the seeds away. However, it is the seed that has the secret of the tree. If someone realized the value of the seeds, he can collect them and plant them. From each seed, another tree can emerge, offering thousands more fruits. Nature has been doing that already. Seeds fall at random places. There are always some places around that have the right combination of conditions where a seed can sprout.

The spiritual masters of India have made giant strides in realizing the Universe within. The entire process of achieving this goal is left to anyone who seeks it. No one is compelled to follow any of these traditions. The majority people in India do not perform Pranayama or Yoga. Many prefer going to temples, offering prayers, ringing the bell, hanging out, participating in festivals, making offerings, taking pictures and going home. But yogis are always respected and revered. If a yogi walks up to a house and begs for alms, food is served or something is offered.

Yogic tradition discourages accumulating wealth however small it might be. The whole focus is on meditation. Yogis spend most of the day in meditation. In order to sustain the body, they need to eat something. They do this by begging. Shiva is shown as a mendicant with a begging bowl. Begging is not considered unworthy in the Indian tradition. Karma can be compensated by offering food to a poor man or a spiritual aspirant. Belief in Karma is deeply entrenched in the system. One is a beggar in his current life in order to pay his Karmic debt. One is doing well because of his good deeds. If he is not aware and abuses his privileged comforts, he too will pay for it. So begging is not considered a sin. Beggars have been around across India since time immemorial. India has been a wealthy land before. It has seen its golden ages. Begging has been an acceptable part of the society all the time. Only they do not call it a status of poverty. Also one cannot tell the difference between a real spiritual master who is walking around begging for alms and one who really is a mendicant. The master might have all the powers to create wealth or perform miracles. Yet they have no tendency to exercise such powers. They remain humble and stay away from the masses most of the time.

With the advent of technology and media, many masters are able to reach to a wider audience across the globe. When one is ready for spiritual advancement, the guru will come. This is a firm belief. If one cannot go to the guru, then the guru will come to help. Interest in Pranayama, Yoga, Chakras etc. have become prevalent in many countries. There are serious practitioners across the globe today. The masters are able to guide them by going abroad and establishing centers for spiritual advancement. It is the need of the hour. If one believed in Karma and reincarnation of the soul, then some people born and brought up outside India have taken to the Indian traditions because of their past life connections. They are born in wealthy nations because of their deeds in the past. They are still reaching out to their roots and are able to connect with those masters who guided them in their past lives. It might also be possible that the conditions in India itself might be changing and the ancient traditions that once survived there may not be able to do so in the long run. Preservation can be possible if those traditions are taken up by others in places, which might become conducive to spiritual growth in the future. The masters have the capability to sense what is ahead due to their powerful intuition and they do just what is needed.

In India one often hears the statement, "Everything happens for a reason." If one's nation is invaded, subjugated and comes out of it, it is a result of past karma of its people. Those who suffered at their hands in the past have come back to return the courtesy. In that process, the culture and consciousness shifts in the right direction. This belief has helped most people in the land to be forgiving and moving along. There are groups of people in India who seek revenge for the past atrocities committed on their ancestors. They are led by power hungry leaders who benefit by stirring up their emotions and benefiting from it. Violence is used as a weapon to target innocents. If they understood the core belief that everything done is a pay back of what has been done before, then they may not feel that vengeful.

If left to itself, the human race discovers values in a roundabout way. It always tends to go the wrong way, realizing the need for correction and then turns around. It is the process of learning. A new change usually triggers it. Every new change is the doorway for a new value system to be realized. However, once the doorway opens, things usually get worse before realization of where we are heading happens. This is how self-discovery works. There are many examples of this. Through all these, communities always had visionaries and seers whose voices initially were sounded out by the noise around. In some societies such people were persecuted.

Europe underwent its own dark ages. The great Roman Empire collapsed. Religious persecution and subjugation prevailed. Many self-realized people were captured and burnt alive as witches and heretics. Power crazy people took over and used every weapon available to them to control others. From within that oppressed system a new age emerged. It took the shape of reform. Then came the renaissance. The telescope was invented. It began to raise questions. The printing press was invented. It sent a shockwave through Europe. Industrial revolution happened. Awareness began to rise. The power of the religious authority was diminished. Through the drama of all these, humans discovered individuality, free thinking and inventions.

Then came the power of the gun. Ships could be built that could survive the rough oceans. The age of exploration began. The vast resources of the world were realized. Exploration transformed into ruthless exploitation. Now it was the turn of non-Europeans to undergo their suffering. Slavery was acknowledged and practiced. World was colonized by tiny nations who had grown powerful through the military technology that had advanced due to industrial revolution and internecine wars. A few centuries later, monarchy became symbolic. Democratic systems began to take hold. Through the process of democratic ideals, rights were realized. Over time, slavery was abolished officially. The world had piled up so much of technology and might that it just exploded from within in the form of two world wars. It led to the formation of the United Nations. Colonialism slowly ended. Those who were ruled were allowed to govern themselves based on ideals developed in the Western nations. World wars brought economic independence to women who had been subjected to secondary role until then.

The world was still divided, polarized between two ideologies that led to further build up of weapons deadlier than ever before. Dictatorships were supported. Weapons were sold. Wars were created. Through all these, the world has discovered more about itself. Racism was ended officially. It might still be in the hearts of many, but in due course that too would change. Environmental safety, animal rights, protection of wildlife, campaign against deforestation, veganism, interest in spirituality, yoga, meditation etc.

have spread across the world. All is not over yet. The world is now divided between dogmatic religions and free thinkers. It will work itself out in due course. It might be violent. But the world will discover newer values on its own.

If one watched all these events, he or she will realize that everything is happening by itself, without anyone controlling it. Changes are all happening from within, through the experience we call as suffering and misery. Sometimes it found a temporary way out of it through violent revolutions that happened in Russia and France. But these did not have lasting effects. People hated them. Power had to be held by force and through subjugation of free will. The collapse of the Soviet Union led to more liberation.

With technological advancement, social media, unimaginable changes are happening in this world. Who could have thought of the Arab Spring? Changes are happening, while the collective karma of many is being worked out in the process. When the karma is paid off, profound changes happen like the collapse of the USSR, independence to countries like India, the end of colonialism, stock market collapse, the Arab Spring and so on. Everything happens for a reason. That reason is based on karma and awareness growing from within.

India has undergone thousands of years of its own golden ages and dark ages. But the core essence of spiritual quest has remained and has been sustained by the sages and yogis. The tradition has remained obscure from the streets and has been preserved over eons. India has that environment from which a Gandhi could emerge. There are many more like him who are not known worldwide. But they are not looking for fame. Nor did Gandhi. However, he became famous because he stood up against the largest empire in the world, using no weapon. Here is the contrast between extremes that is so characteristics of the land. The mighty empire that had become powerful because of military technology, with all its weapons and power, confronted a man who stood up with no weapons and used non-violence as his method. In 1947, when India was finally given its independence from colonialism, the spiritual power of India won. For two hundred years, this huge land of empires and kingdoms was ruled by a nation that was considerably smaller in size and was far away. It appears odd that a small nation could rule a huge continent and beyond. But it happened. India underwent all its struggle and subjugation because of the collective karma of its denizens in the past. All karma has to be worked out before changes happen for the good. Those who are subjugated return to subjugate. That is the law of karma.

If one looked at the history of every land, a similar phenomenon can be discerned. For 70 years, the people of Russia and Eastern Europe suffered under the staggering weight of communism and tyranny. But one day, it all disappeared like the morning fog. The wall in Berlin was broken and it symbolized the end of communistic rule. Collective karma causes beings to descend and work their karmic debts through. Liberation comes only when one is free of karma. One can feel relaxation only when pain is completely gone. The job of pain is to restrict and prevent over exertion. It is there to protect. But it is undesirable. So is karma. It protects so that one does not over exert and go in a direction that harms himself and everyone around. The natural tendency in every being is to be free of restrictions and limitations.

The Hindu systems generally do not give much importance to detailed record keeping of historical events. Because of the impermanence of the mortal life and due to the belief in reincarnation, keeping track of history is felt unimportant. Human history mostly dwells on bad memories. Old memories are kept alive to be used for future conflicts. If life and death are cycles, then one can be born on the side of the enemy in one life. If he is not aware, he could inherit more karma as a result. Everything made by humans becomes a remnant and ruin as time goes on. Empires have come and gone. During every empire, kings came and ruled, waged wars, conquered lands, gave alms and charity, built temples and monuments and died. Then another invader came and took over. This is the same pattern, much similar to humans being born in a household, living, dying and being replaced by someone else. No one has a record of what the ancestor's name a thousand generations ago was. For a spiritual goal, impermanence of materialistic world is recognized and not given much importance as a result.

Though one claims that the knowledge of history is important in order not to repeat the mistakes of the past, knowledge of history has been used mostly to kindle more fire and violence in the future. The only difference is that the past is being repeated by new people to settle old scores of the ancestors using new weapons. Wars have been fought in the past. There has been enough history of it. If history has really prevented people from repeating past mistakes, have wars stopped happening? Wars have become deadlier and more destructive. Fear and panic have only increased. History is good if it does not dwell on the negative. Unfortunately the human mind tends to like the negative more because it gives an opportunity to feel victimized and seek revenge. The Hindu systems instead maintained what is known as Puranas where the emphasis was mostly on the good deeds and lessons learned. Reading the ruins might give some knowledge to the archeologists in addition to name, fame and museum displays. When a system is directed towards spiritual induction, then its emphasis is away from anything materialistic. It is customary to donate one's wealth and jewelry to the deity in a temple.

The single letter chant "Aum" is heard all across India. Aum links the inner spirit with the Universe. Chanting internally helps intensify the awareness of that link. When someone sees a Ganesh statue while walking on the street, his mind anchors to the Aum sound, which Ganesh symbolizes. Animals on the street are all set up as symbols to link with the Universal consciousness subliminally. By giving them an important role in every mythical story, the inner mind gets trained to accept them as vehicles of transcendence from the ordinary to the extraordinary state. Every deity is depicted as riding one such vehicle. One must try not to interpret the image literally, but transcend that image to understand the spiritual purpose behind it. It happens as one lives continuously in such an environment learning tolerance and becoming philosophical through the vicissitudes in life.

In some people transcendence occurs subliminally. It is important to have this slow and subliminal transition into a higher dimension. Otherwise such an experience can be shocking to an individual. We grow from childhood to adulthood slowly and imperceptibly. If we transitioned abruptly, we can undergo a transition that will not be comfortable. We can have an adult body and the mindset of a child. Changes have to be imperceptible and the development of spiritual awareness gradual. That is why the street level spiritual training turns into a religious practice where guidance happens through a social upbringing. Once one matures spiritually, provided they have that inner goal and desire, then they automatically will pursue more rigorous practices.

Most people remain at the street level of spirituality. And no one can take that right away from them. It is entirely up to each individual to choose to do what they like. Most have the natural tendency to stay on the street where crows, rodents, snakes, monkeys, cows and sometimes elephants come and go. The ones, who sense a difference between their awareness and that of the other animals on the street, take the first step into the temple. Having been used to the street, it is hard for them to suddenly switch and turn their attention towards the temple. The street is still attractive. That is where "life" is. It is noisy. It is boisterous. It is lively and colorful. It is full of movement and energy. So many just go back into the street.

Some sense something different between the temple and the street. Whatever is projected on the temple walls does not make much sense. There is no one to explain to them what all it means. Wouldn't it be nice if someone sat at the entrance and explained all that? That would be what we call as a tour guide. A tour guide explains everything, collects your money and you are back on the street. You take some pictures to remember and no one cares after a few years. But if one began to gain an understanding of what is projected on the walls of the temple by his own inner contemplation, it becomes a lot more interesting. He realizes that someone has been there and has left all these symbols to convey an experience that is not easily discernable from the street. Noise blocks the subtle sounds from being heard. If one takes away the noise slowly, then more sensations hitherto ignored begin to surface.

As one goes deeper and deeper into the temple, what is projected around begins to connect more and what appeared like a secretive nonsense, begins to make sense. Everything is learned best when experienced first hand. It is for everyone to experience to know the reality and not through descriptions and explanations from others. At the street level, may be some of it is needed. But once one steps into the temple, he will be drawn slowly towards the inner sanctum as the reality will begin to reveal itself. Awareness grows and one realizes that everything has been there all along. But only through inner experience he is becoming aware of it.

Only someone having an artistic taste will stop and admire the artwork in a gallery. If someone is blind, it may not matter to him. He might walk through the art gallery and look for the toilet, which is his basic need at the moment. A lot of people are walking through life without realizing what it has to offer. Most are focused only on their basic needs and there is enough distraction to take their time and attention away when they get time. That is the modern world today. However, all is not lost. The traditions of India have survived through the ages and direct onslaught on many occasions. The world is beginning to realize the gifts it has to offer and benefit from it. There is no religion involved at what is being offered, though it comes from the Hindu religious system. No one can own copyrights on them. They are for the betterment of humanity and anyone seeking increased spiritual awareness is entitled to seek it and benefit from it.

India is credited with giving the world "Nothing". And it is a profound concept. One who has spiritual awakening will see everything in it. To get there, one needs the drama of life. In reality no one is undergoing spiritual progress. All that is happening is an increased awareness of his spirituality. By going through the pages of this book, I hope I have given some insight into the essence of a system that appears chaotic and complex from a distance. The elephant can appear differently to different people if they are blindfolded. I have given my views of it and it might be different from that of others. All views only enhance the overall experience. Some of what I have mentioned is from what I have heard and read. Some of it is from my own inner experience. If "Hinduism" no longer appears exotic to you after reading this work, then I can say I have achieved my purpose. I see myself playing the role of a milestone that points towards a certain direction. I have not tried to guide anyone. I pray that you have absorbed some essence from these pages and enhance your own enhancement of spiritual awareness. May you be blessed!

REFERENCE

1. Freedom At Midnight – Dominic Lapierre and Larry Collins

2. Aghora – the Left Handed Path - Svoboda

3. Living with Kundalini – Gopi Krishna

4. A passage to secret India – Paul Brunton

5. Autobiography of a yogi – Paramahamsa Yogananda

6. Walking with the Himalayan masters – Swami Rama

7. The Bhagavat Gita – Paramahamsa Yogananda

8. The path of fire and light – Swami Rama

9. Tantra Unveiled – Pundit Rajamani Tigunait

ABOUT THE AUTHOR

Partha Rajagopal is an Indian American, living in Portland, Oregon since 1986. He has a PhD in engineering. He has worked in many engineering areas for close to 30 years. Having been brought up in a changing world around, he has had the opportunity to observe many things that came from the ancient traditions of India as well as those that kept arising in the modern world. He is presenting some of that learning in this book.

http://shop.simhaartworks.com/

http://www.etsy.com/shop/simhaartworks

http://simhaartworks.storenvy.com/

Dr. Partha also is a trained and certified Hypnotherapist. He is an artist and a writer. Samples of his pencil art and links are here.

Printed in Great Britain
by Amazon

86405504R00132